What God Has Joined Together

Biblical Foundations for Marriage

Tim Hegg

Contents

Chapter 1: Male & Female: Some Basics..........................4

Chapter 2: Male & Female: The Effects of Sin 17

Chapter 3: Marriage as a Covenant 29

Chapter 4: Marriage as a Covenant, Part 2 39

Chapter 5: Characteristics of a Godly Husband 49

Chapter 6: Characteristics of a Godly Wife.................... 67

Chapter 7: Betrothal & Marriage..................................... 97

Chapter 8: Marriage in a Fallen World: Divorce 125

Chapter 9: Knowing How to Forgive, and Doing It 145

Chapter 10: Husband & Wife: Intimate Friends............ 165

Chapter 1
Male & Female: Some Basics

Introduction

Created in God's Image, Gen 1:26–28

> Gen. 1:26 Then God said, "Let Us make man in Our image, according to Our likeness; and let them rule over the fish of the sea and over the birds of the sky and over the cattle and over all the earth, and over every creeping thing that creeps on the earth." 27 God created man in His own image, in the image of God He created him; male and female He created them. 28 God blessed them; and God said to them, "Be fruitful and multiply, and fill the earth, and subdue it; and rule over the fish of the sea and over the birds of the sky and over every living thing that moves on the earth."

The word translated "image" is צֶלֶם, *tzelem,* which is used, for instance, of statues carved or molded to look like a person or an animal. In fact, the word is used in connection with idols made in the "image" of pagan gods (cf. Num 33:52 Ezek 7:20, cp. Amos 5:26). The word here denotes that God created man to resemble Him—to "look like" Him.

Next the text tells us that God made man in His "likeness," which is the Hebrew word דְּמוּת, *d'mut.* This word also denotes "likeness," but more in the sense of a general outline or shape. Whereas *tzelem* speaks to a likeness that has a clear correspondence to the original, *d'mut* is less exact. *D'mut* denotes just a general similarity, whereas *tzelem* would emphasize a close resemblance.

The fact that the two terms are used in parallel here would indicate that the second word, *d'mut,* helps to further define *tzelem.* Since God is a spirit, and does not have physical form, it is impossible to say that mankind was created "to look like" God. The additional word, *d'mut,* helps us to understand Moses' meaning: mankind was created with characteristics that directly parallel the characteristics of God. We are created in His image in the sense that we are like Him in some very important ways.

This is illustrated later in Genesis. Note Gen 5:1-3. Once again,

Moses reminds us that God created mankind "in His image, according to His likeness" (v. 1). Then note how the same words are used in v. 3:

> When Adam had lived one hundred and thirty years, he became the father of a son in his own likeness (*d'mut*), according to his image (*tzelem*), and named him Seth.

Now we get a better picture: Seth was like his father Adam—he shared the same basic characteristics of his father and mother, but was obviously different in that he was a distinct individual. He most likely looked like his father, and anyone looking at him could tell that he was part of Adam and Chavah's family. In addition, he had the same general characteristics of his parents—he was clearly human, not part of the animal kingdom.

So the first thing we learn about ourselves is this: *Being created in the image and likeness of God means that we share some very important characteristics with our Creator.*

Mankind = Male & Female

If we look again at Gen 1:26–28 we see a second important fact: when the Scriptures say that God created "man" in His image, it means He created *mankind* in His image, not just Adam.

> Gen. 1:26 Then God said, "Let Us make man in Our image, according to Our likeness; and let them rule over the fish of the sea and over the birds of the sky and over the cattle and over all the earth, and over every creeping thing that creeps on the earth." 27 God created man in His own image, in the image of God He created him; male and female He created them. 28 God blessed them; and God said to them, "Be fruitful and multiply, and fill the earth, and subdue it; and rule over the fish of the sea and over the birds of the sky and over every living thing that moves on the earth."

Note the following:
- God creates "man" (אָדָם, *adam* = "mankind") and says, "let *them* rule...." Thus, mankind is comprised of a male and female.
- In v. 27, it says "God created man (*adam*) in His own image, in the image of God He create *him*, male and female He created *them.* Here, mankind is viewed as an absolute unity and can be referred to in the singular: "...He created *him.*" Yet the text goes on to say "male and female, He created *them.*"

What do we learn from this? We learn that mankind is made up of both male and female, and that alone, neither the male nor the female can represent mankind. Only in the relationship of male and female is mankind complete. In the basic structure of God's created universe, men and women are *mutually dependent* upon each other in order to realize and display the image of God in which they were created.

Secondly, since mankind was created in God's image or likeness, and since mankind is comprised of both male and female, this means that both men and women are created in God's image. This means that in God's creative order, *both men and women share equally in the glory and responsibility of bearing God's image.*

Thirdly, v. 28 says that "God blessed *them*." This blessing comes upon both the male and female, and is seen in:
- Their ability to "be fruitful and multiply and fill the earth"
- Their duty to "subdue and rule" over the earth.

Once again, we find some very important points in this opening paragraph. First, male and female are equally blessed by God. This means that each plays an essential role in fulfilling God's purpose as His image bearers. Neither male nor female can accomplish their created roles alone—they must work together. This is first expressed in obeying the command to "be fruitful and multiply, and fill the earth." God ordained that children should come from the union of male and female together.

Secondly, the ability to subdue and rule over the earth is dependent upon male and female working together. The Creator gave this responsibility to mankind, not just Adam or Chavah. Once again, in order to realize the very purpose for which they were created, male and female must consider themselves partners mutually dependent upon each other in accomplishing the task of ruling over the earth.

What is the Image of God in Mankind?

One of the obvious "surprises" in our text (Gen 1:26–28, also cf. Gen 3:22; 11:17) is that God presents Himself in the plural: "…let *us* make man in *our* image, according to *our* likeness…" (v. 26). Yet in the next verse, Moses speaks of God in the singular: "God created man in *His* own image, in the image of God *He* created him; male and female *He* created them." Through the ages a number of suggestions have been offered to account for this. The Sages consider the plurals to be speaking of God and the angels (cf. Mid. Rab. *Gen.* 8:3). But one can hardly consider what might be meant by creating mankind in the image of the angels! In fact, the only explanation that is consistent with the text itself is to understand that in some mysterious way, God is a plurality within an infinite and eternal oneness or unity. There is only one true God—yet He has revealed Himself to us as a plurality: as Father (e.g., Is 63:16; 64:8), as Messiah (e.g., Is 9:6), and as Spirit (e.g., Gen 1:2; Ex 31:3; Num 24:2).

It is this very aspect of God's essential character that is the fundamental characteristic of the image of God in mankind. Even as God is revealed to us as Father, Messiah, and Spirit, yet is one, so mankind was created as male and female with the ability also to be one within the context of the covenant of marriage.

> For this reason a man shall leave his father and his mother, and be joined
> to his wife; and they shall become one flesh. (Gen 2:24)

This ability to be diverse yet one is not merely seen in the act of procreation, though surely children are the most obvious proof of being "one flesh." In even greater ways, this unity in the midst of diversity is also demonstrated in companionship, serving each other, and finding true meaning and satisfaction in the love-relationship of marriage.

This is not to imply that only those who are married display the image of God! Rather, it is in the covenant of marriage that the image of God is most clearly seen as the union of diverse mankind. Yet in the context of community, the fundamental family unit, and the relationships of mutual love and service expressed in this relationship, is extended in measure to the whole community. Since in some ways the community functions as a family (expressing companionship, service to one another, and deriving true meaning and satisfaction from this relationship), those who are single within the community also have the opportunity to express oneness in the face of diversity, displaying the image of God in which all mankind is created.

Let's Summarize

- Being created in the image of God means that we share some very important characteristics with our Creator

- God created mankind in His image, according to His likeness, and mankind consists of male and female.

- This means that both men and women bear the image of God.

- One fundamental characteristic that we share with our Creator is the ability to be diverse yet to be one.

- In marriage, the unity of male and female is most obviously seen in their children.

- The deeper reality of oneness in marriage is seen in companionship, serving each other, and in finding meaning and satisfaction in the love-relationship of husband and wife.

- This ability to be many yet one is also seen in the larger family context of community.

It is Not Good for Man to be Alone

The structure of Gen 1–2 is important for us to understand if we hope to properly interpret these opening words of Scripture. As is typical of ancient Hebrew thought and writing, Moses tells us the story of creation with a particular emphasis in mind. His desire is to show that mankind is the pinnacle of God's creation—that mankind functions as God's vice-regent over the earth.

To do this, Moses gives us the creation account in two ways: first, he gives us the overall picture—the whole story, in Gen 1. Then, in Gen 2, he narrows his scope to look particularly at the creation of mankind. We might use a microscope as an illustration. When one first prepares to look at something through a microscope, he uses the less powerful lens to gain the widest possible perspective. Then, having pinpointed the object he wishes to investigate more closely, he turns the lens to a higher power to zero in on that object. In like manner, Gen 1 gives the broad perspective, and Gen 2 narrows the scope to the creation of mankind. This is why Gen 1 speaks of God creating mankind as male and female (1:26-28). When we come to Gen 2, Moses gives us the details of exactly how mankind was created, and even more, the purpose for which mankind was created.

In 2:7 we read:

> Then the Lord God formed man of dust from the ground, and breathed into his nostrils the breath of life; and man became a living being.

From this we learn several important things:

- man was created from the dust of the ground, meaning that he did not possess the ability to sustain himself. He is made of materials already created by God
- God breathed into man the breath of life (נִשְׁמַת חַיִּים, *nishmat chayim*) and then he became a living being (נֶפֶשׁ חַיָּה, *nefesh chayah*). Man is the only created being who received the breath of life directly from God. In this way, he is set apart from the other living creatures (animals) that God created. This in turn symbolized that the life given to man was directly connected to the Giver of life. Man shares in the very life of his Creator

The detailed story of God's activity in creating mankind goes on to describe how God planted a garden and put man into the garden to cultivate and keep it:

> Then the Lord God took the man and put him into the garden of Eden to cultivate it and keep it. (Gen 2:15)

God also gave the man a commandment regarding what he could eat, and what he could not eat. All the fruit of the trees were for his food, but one tree, the tree of the knowledge of good and evil, was strictly off limits. In placing man into the garden as His appointed ruler, God also gave commandments by which man's success as His ruler over the garden would be achieved. This demonstrated that man's success in his appointed tasks as keeper of God's garden would require maintaining a relationship of obedience with his Maker.

Yet immediately following the man's appointment as keeper of God's garden, the following notice is given:

> Then the Lord God said, "It is not good for the man to be alone; I will make him a helper suitable for him." (Gen 2:18)

This is the first time in the creation narrative that God declares something "not good." Everything else that He saw was good or even very good. The fact that Moses gives us this "not good" notice immediately following God's instructions to the man regarding his role as keeper of the garden, indicates why man being alone was not good: *as a lone individual he was unable to accomplish the task that God had given him.*

Surely God knew this would be the case! Then why did He create man and put him in the garden when it was known he could not succeed in the task as long as he was alone? We can only speculate, but it may well be that God did so in order to teach man that he could not accomplish the task for which he was created unless he had help. Self-reliance and independence are contrary to God's creative order for mankind. As the image bearer of God, mankind could only accomplish his role as God's vice-regent upon the earth by living out an inter-dependence which demonstrated a unity in the midst of diversity.

The second part of Gen 2:18 notes God's intention to make a "helper" suitable for man. The word "helper" is עֵזֶר (*'ezer*), which means "one who gives assistance or help" and is used of God as the helper of mankind (Ex 18:4; Deut 33:7, 29; Ps 20:3; 115:9–11; 121:2; 124:8;

146:5; Dan 11:34). This being the case, the designation "helper" cannot be viewed as an inferior position. Rather, one who is able to help is one who comes from a position of strength. God intended to create a helper for man because he lacked something essential which the helper could supply. Together they could accomplish the role of God's vice-regent over the earth, something man could not do by himself.

Note that the helper would be "suitable for him." Actually, the Hebrew is כְּנֶגְדּוֹ (*k'negdo*), which literally is "corresponding to him," or "opposite him" in the sense of a mirror image. The helper God intended to create was one who would be his partner, equally sharing the attributes of God's image.

So was woman created in order to help man achieve his purpose? Or to put it another way, does woman only find her creative purpose in relationship to helping man? This, in fact, has been a predominate interpretation of our text throughout the history of the Christian Church. But when taken within the fuller context of the creation narrative, such an interpretation cannot stand. In Gen 1 it is clear that mankind is made up of both male and female. God's plan always included both Adam and Chavah as the first of mankind. So woman was not created as an addition for man, but God's plan, from the beginning, was that man and woman would together accomplish God's purpose for them as His vice-regent upon the earth.

This is further illustrated in the following context of Gen 2. After stating that "it is not good for man to be alone," the notice is given that God brought the animals He had created in order that Adam should name each of them. Since in the Hebrew perspective, a name bespeaks essential characteristics, the exercise of naming the animals should be understood as Adam investigating each animal closely, no doubt with the purpose of finding a way to overcome his being "alone." Yet, according to v. 20, there was not found an *'ezer k'negdo,* "a helper corresponding to him."

Once again, the order of the text gives us God's intention to create such a helper before Adam is given the task of naming the animals. Apparently the naming task is given to Adam to show him that none of the animals correspond to him. Or to put it simply, God gave the task of naming the animals to Adam so that he would realize that only the one God created as his partner could overcome the dilemma of "being alone." There was no essential companionship in the animal kingdom. Thus, woman is created, not to make up what is lacking in Adam, but as an essential partner together with him.

The creation of woman (vv. 21 ff) thus becomes the crowning act of God's creation. While Adam was formed from the dust (v. 7), God formed Chavah from a rib taken from Adam (מִצַּלְעֹתָיו), after putting Adam in a deep sleep. As the master Surgeon, God heals the incision immediately, then forms the woman from Adam's rib.

What are we to understand from this? First, woman corresponds directly to man because she is derived from him. Secondly, the rib bone is from the region of the body which, from a Hebrew perspective, houses one's deepest thoughts and emotions (the heart). Thus woman would correspond to man in far more than mere physical likeness—she would share the human qualities necessary for companionship, mutual service, and life's meaning. Some have noted that God did not take bone from Adam's skull, as though woman would rule over him, nor from his foot, as though he would subdue her in servitude, but from his side, a picture of companionship and protection. Finally, the emphasis expressed in the fact that Chavah is formed from Adam's rib is that they would always be connected in a mysterious union of oneness. Man had learned that he could not be alone, and that he therefore needed woman. Woman was to learn that she too was dependent upon man, for her very origin was from him.

The scene portrayed in our text, of God bringing Chavah to Adam, sets up the divinely ordained relationship of marriage. Like the father who grants a man the right to marry his daughter, so God brings Chavah to Adam. Upon seeing her, he immediately recognizes the direct correspondence to himself, which he did not find in any of the other created creatures. His first words about woman are, fittingly, poetic:

> This is now bone of my bones,
> And flesh of my flesh;
> She shall be called Woman,
> Because she was taken out of Man. (Gen 2:23)

We may note several things from Adam's words. First, the word "now" could better be understood as "this time" (זֹאת הַפַּעַם, z'ot hapa'am). The task of naming the animals is still fresh in Adam's mind. Of the many animals he named, none were found suitable. But "this time" things were different! Secondly, Adam immediately recognizes that this one whom God had fashioned was in direct correspondence to himself.

"Flesh and bone" is a Hebrew merism, standing for the whole person. In essence he says, "she is essentially like me." Thirdly, the naming process for woman is quite different than it was for the animals. Here, Adam does not give the woman a personal name, but a generic title, "woman" (אִשָּׁה, *'ishah*), sounding very much like his own generic title, "man" (אִישׁ, *'ish*). This is the first time Adam is called a "man"—up to this point in the Genesis record, where our English translations have the word "man," it is translating the Hebrew אָדָם, *'adam,* a word that sounded much like אֲדָמָה, *'adamah,* "ground," the substance from which Adam was formed. In the same way, Adam plays on the similar sounds of Hebrew *'ish* and *'ishah,* the words for "man" and "woman." Just like *'adam* was formed from *'adamah,* so *'ishah* was formed from *'ish.*

What are we to derive from this naming ceremony, and the first appearance of the Hebrew words for "man" and "woman?" First, in giving the generic title "woman," and taking the generic title "man," Adam is indicating their equality. They are different, that is certain. But in their essential nature and being, they are equal. Secondly, since this is the first time the word *'ish,* "man" is found, we may also note that Adam discovers his manhood only when he faces the woman, the one created by God to be his partner in life. They are different, yet the same. They are two who will become one.

This most profound reality gives rise to Moses' theological statement regarding the relationship between man and woman.

> For this reason a man shall leave his father and his mother, and be joined to his wife; and they shall become one flesh. (v. 24)

Moses begins, "For this reason," but to what exactly is he referring? What is the reason that underlies his next statement? It seems clear that he is referring to the equality of male and female as possessing the same human character, and the nearness of the woman to the man since she was taken from him. In other words, Moses' statement here tells us something very important: it will be the natural inclination of man and woman to be drawn to each other. Moreover, so strong will they be drawn to each other, that they will willingly leave the protection and support of parents to form a oneness of their own.

It is to this God-given attraction between the man and woman that the final verse of Gen 2 speaks: "And the man and his wife were both naked and were not ashamed" (v. 25). The attraction that they felt toward each other was not tainted with any kind of selfishness. They did not view each other as an object to be controlled or conquered, nor were they concerned about self-fulfillment. As long as their relationship with the Creator remained unbroken, "the pristine innocence and dignity of sexuality was not despoiled" (Sarna, *JPS Torah Commentary: Genesis,* p. 23).

This is very important, because it teaches us that the physical relationship between man and woman was, from the beginning, considered to be something holy and good. Only when sexuality is taken outside of the boundaries declared holy by God does it loose its beauty and purpose.

Let's Summarize

- God created man out of the "dust of the ground." Then He breathed into him the breath of life and he became a living soul. God's direct breath of life makes man distinct from the animals because man shares the very life of God.

- After creating Adam, God put him in charge of a garden He had planted. This indicates that mankind's role on this earth is directly related to being God's workman.

- God gave a commandment to Adam regarding which trees he could use for food and one from which he could not eat. This emphasizes the truth that man will only be able to accomplish the tasks for which he was created when he obeys God.

- Throughout the creation story, God continually proclaims that what He had made was "good." Yet after creating Adam, He declared "it is *not* good for man to be alone." We learn from this that Adam, by himself, could not fulfill the task God had given him. This is because God never intended man to be alone. But man had to understand that he needed help.

- God created woman from a rib taken from man. This stresses woman's essential equality with man in terms of personhood and worth.

- The woman is called a "suitable helper." This means that she alone fulfills the role of an equal partner.

- When Adam saw Chavah, he immediately recognized that she was a person like himself with whom he could have true companionship.

- The fact that man and woman were created by God with the same essential human characteristics forms the basis for God's design in marriage.

Talk About It!

1. Go over the ideas presented here regarding the essential meaning of the "image of God" in mankind. How should this govern the perspective men and women have of each other?

2. When men "put down women," or when women "put down men," how is this also a degrading of God's work?

3. Do you think sometimes men look at women as inferior? Do women sometimes look at men as inferior? Why do you think this is so?

4. Is it just a myth, or do men often think they don't need any help? If as men, we act as though we do not need any help, how does this reflect on God's statement that "it is not good for man to be alone?"

5. Discuss this question: "What characteristics make a truly good friend or companion?"

6. God's order for marriage is that a man should leave his father and mother and be joined to his wife. Discuss:
   a. what can the parents do to hinder this process?
   b. what can the parents do to aid this process?
   c. what can the man and woman do to make this process difficult?

    d.   what can the man and woman do to make this process meaningful and good?

Chapter 2
Male & Female: The Effects of Sin

The opening chapters of Genesis present us with a picture of Adam and Chavah as partners together in the enterprise of mankind. Each were created by the hand of God, and each recognized in each other their God-ordained complement. Their role as God's servants in tending His garden was done with mutual respect and care. So perfect was this relationship that Moses concludes chapter 2 with the notice that "the man and his wife were both naked and were not ashamed." In the most intimate aspects of their companionship, there was no hint of selfishness. Each was for the other in a wholesome and holy manner.

But this idyllic relationship was about to change. Rebellion and sin against God would alter their relationship with each other as well. The strengths of each would become a snare, and their weaknesses would be exploited. The notice in chapter 2 that "it is not good for man to be alone" would now return as a factor, in spite of the fact that each was created for the other. In the fracture of their relationship, Adam and Chavah would believe that it was okay to be alone—that one's own desires were a priority over the needs of the other.

Satan's Scheme

As we have already noted, the image of God in mankind is vested most strategically within the male/female relationship. As God Himself is plural yet one ("let us make man in our image"), so the oneness of Adam and Chavah enabled them to portray this mysterious yet vital image of their Creator. It is not surprising, then, that in the scheme of the evil one, his goal is to disrupt this oneness between man and woman, and in so doing, to render ineffective their ability to portray the image of their Creator. Satan's goal is to negate the very purpose for which we were created.

Satan's plan followed a well crafted formula: 1) discredit God in order to break the trusting relationship that mankind had with Him, which in turn would 2) hinder the interdependence of mankind through selfish motivations. Take note: this is still the enemy's battle plan!

When Satan can turn our hearts from God, he has also succeeded in turning our hearts against each other. This is because in turning from God, one turns only to oneself, and such self-centeredness destroys interpersonal relationships. Thus, the battle plan to be victorious over our enemy must be first to draw near to God with a humble heart, which in turn enables us to love others.

Has God Said?

The Deceiver came to Chavah with his lies. The first words from the Enemy are "Has God said…?" Now he is not asking whether God has spoken with Adam and Chavah, but whether they should trust Him to have told the truth. The first attack upon mankind is to suggest that God is not good. And if God is not good, then He cannot be trusted. Moreover, if God cannot be trusted, then mankind must view themselves as independent from God, as God's judge.

Here is the foundational question: do we receive what God has said on the basis of faith that He is eternally and infinitely good, or do we view ourselves as in a position to judge the motivations of God, whether they are righteous or selfish? Our starting point makes all the difference in the world! For if we begin with the premise that God is good, then we immediately accept that what He has said to us is also good and worthy of our obedience. Moreover, starting with the presupposition that God is good means that we are dependent upon Him, for we await His communication to us as the basis for knowing who we are and what we are to do as His created servants. The converse is also true. If we begin with the possibility that God may not be good (or at least not good all of the time), then we immediately take up a position of independence from Him, for we feel it is our duty to judge what He says and does. We therefore may consider ourselves as either autonomous (independent) or dependent upon God.

Of course, the reality is that we are dependent upon God, but we, like Adam and Chavah, may believe the lie that we are independent and that our lives are ours to govern. How we see ourselves (as dependent or independent) will make a great difference in how we form and maintain relationships with others.

Is God Good?

Satan's question to Chavah is formulated to bring into question

God's goodness: "Indeed, has God said, 'You shall not eat from any tree of the garden'?" (Gen 3:1) How unloving and unkind of God to prohibit His servants from eating food from the garden! Satan turns the matter on its head: God has given every tree save one to Adam and Chavah for food! Satan suggests that God has given them nothing.

After Chavah explains that every tree was given to them for food, except for the tree of the knowledge of good and evil, and that the penalty for eating from this tree was death, Satan counters: "You surely will not die! For God knows that in the day you eat from it your eyes will be opened, and you will be like God, knowing good and evil." His point is that if Adam and Chavah were to disobey God, they would realize that they have the ability to discern good and evil on their own, without His help. In other words, they would realize an independence from God that made them equal with Him. Moreover, Satan implies that had God told them the whole story, they would realize that they really didn't need Him. God had hidden the truth from them in order to maintain His "upper hand."

We all know the story: Chavah saw in the fruit something desirable: "When the woman saw that the tree was good for food, and that it was a delight to the eyes, and that the tree was desirable to make one wise, she took from its fruit and ate; and she gave also to her husband with her, and he ate" (3:6). Here we discover several important things. First, Adam and Chavah, as created beings, were given the ability to use creation against God. He had created their appetites. He had created their eyes. God had given them intellectual ability. These were good. But here the appetite and the eyes along with the desire for wisdom are used selfishly. The self-centered question of "what's good for me" coupled with an acceptance of Satan's lies, had become the priority.

The fact that Adam and Chavah had disobeyed God in taking from the prohibited tree meant that they now, in fact, did *know* good and evil. Previously they had an intellectual understanding of evil, for in receiving the prohibition regarding the tree, and understanding that the penalty for transgression was death, they understood the difference between obedience and disobedience—between life and death. But now they had become intimately acquainted with evil. It was no longer a thought or concept—it had become a part of them.

The very first effect of their sin was that they no longer looked at each other the same as before: "Then the eyes of both of them were opened, and they knew that they were naked; and they sewed fig leaves together and made themselves loin coverings" (3:7). Whereas before each one saw in the other the beauty of God's handiwork, they now saw each other through new eyes of selfishness.

When God comes looking for them, and confronts them with regard to their nakedness, each gives an excuse: Adam blames Chavah, and Chavah blames the serpent. Once again, self-preservation rules.

The New Pattern of Male/Female Relationship

The text of Genesis now turns to a description of the results flowing from Adam and Chavah's disobedience. The serpent is cursed, along with the ground upon which he will crawl. Dust would be the food of the serpent, and thorns would grow up from ground, spoiling the efforts of even the best gardener. But most important for our study are the words of God regarding Adam and Chavah, and the effect of sin upon their individual tendencies, and their relationship together.

We will look first at 3:16 —

To the woman He said,	אֶל־הָאִשָּׁה אָמַר
"I will greatly multiply	הַרְבָּה אַרְבֶּה
Your pain in childbirth,	עִצְּבוֹנֵךְ וְהֵרֹנֵךְ
In pain you will bring forth children;	בְּעֶצֶב תֵּלְדִי בָנִים
Yet your desire will be for your husband,	וְאֶל־אִישֵׁךְ תְּשׁוּקָתֵךְ
And he will rule over you."	וְהוּא יִמְשָׁל־בָּךְ

Note a few important things from this text:

1. The woman's pain would be related to childbearing. Later, in vv. 17–19, Adam's "pain" relates to his work as a tiller of the ground. For both, what was given as a joy (children, one's work) would now be mixed with pain and sorrow.
2. God does not curse either Adam or Chavah. He only curses the serpent and the ground. The results of sin that would be experienced by Adam and Chavah are therefore not a curse of God, but the inevitable result of rebellion against God.

3. The English translations take liberty in translating the Hebrew *vav* conjunction (often translated "and"), used three times in this text.

    a. In the phrase "Your pain in childbirth," the Hebrew has (literally) "your pain, even (and) your childbirth." In this case, the *vav* is most likely pleonastic ("even").
    b. Opening the line "Your desire will be for your husband." NASB translates the *vav* as "Yet" (contrastive)
    c. Opening the last line: "And he will rule over you."

However, there are other legitimate options for translating the conjunctions of the last two lines.

One of the important keys to understanding this important verse is the word "desire" (תְּשׁוּקָה, *teshuqah*). This word is found only three times in the Tanach: Gen 3:16; 4:7; Song 7:11. While its occurrence in Song of Songs may well have sexual desire as its meaning, the other usage (Gen 4:7), being in such close proximity to our text, and having a parallel structure to it, is very informative:

…sin is crouching at the door;	לַפֶּתַח חַטָּאת רֹבֵץ
and its desire is for you,	וְאֵלֶיךָ תְּשׁוּקָתוֹ
but you must master it."	וְאַתָּה תִּמְשָׁל־בּוֹ

Here we discover that "desire" (תְּשׁוּקָה) means "to dominate," "to control." Sin was "crouching at the door," like a lion waiting to overpower Cain if he were to walk out. Yet the admonition to him is that he "must rule (מָשַׁל, *mashal*) over it" meaning "conquer" or "subdue." This is precisely the same word (מָשַׁל) used in the last line of 3:16, "and he will rule over you." Except for the change of pronouns, these two lines are identical.

Now, if this same sense of "desire" is to be understood in 3:16, we would derive this meaning of the final two clauses:

So you will desire to dominate your husband,
But he will subdue you.

The increased pain in childbirth would cause the wife to seek security and help from her husband. Yet fearing that he would not aid her in the time of her pain, she would seek to dominate him, to control him in order to assure his assistance. Yet the reality is that he would not be controlled, but would himself subdue or rule over his wife.

The entrance of sin into the lives of Adam and Chavah, and through them, to all mankind, has caused a complete reversal of their created roles. Whereas Chavah was created as an *'ezer* (helper), someone to come to Adam's aid and supply in him what he was lacking, now the woman would seek to dominate and control the man. And though Adam originally viewed Chavah as "bone of my bone and flesh of my flesh," meaning he saw her as his equal, and the companion together with whom he could fulfill his role as God's servant, now she is someone to be conquered or subdued. Whereas before the rebellion against God, man and woman viewed each other as equals, partnered together to accomplish God's designs, now their independence would evidence itself in seeking the good of oneself at the expense of the other.

We may rightly ask the question how the woman would think to dominate or control her husband, and how the husband would "win" the battle by subduing his wife. Clearly, the man was created with greater physical strength than the woman. Peter, writing to husbands in the believing community, exhorts them to "live with your wives in an understanding way, as with someone weaker, since she is a woman" (1Pet 3:7). Here the language indicates he has in mind her physical weakness. So the woman could not have thought she could dominate her husband physically. Rather, the woman would use other means to control and dominate. But in spite of her best efforts at controlling her husband, the reality would be that, because of his physical strength, he would have the upper hand. What is described here is nothing short of a war, where both parties lose!

Is there any hope, then, for male and female to return to that place of equality and mutual companionship which they had before the fall into sin? The answer is given in the promise of a Redeemer, which preceded the description of woman and man vying for self preservation.

Note Genesis 3:15, the initial promise given to Chavah—

> And I will put enmity
> Between you and the woman,

And between your seed and her seed;
He shall bruise you on the head,
And you shall bruise him on the heel.

The promise of One who was to come was also a promise of a way out of the domain of sin that had engulfed mankind. He would do battle with Satan, and would prevail, because though He would be wounded in the process, He would inevitably deal a fatal blow to the head of the enemy. Thus, in the redemption provided by the Promised One, man and woman are enabled to overcome the effects of the rebellion into which they had come, and return to a companionship in the service of their Creator.

Yet the effects of sin, both in the world and in the sinful nature, remain. The companionship of husband and wife would only be possible through the spiritual struggle of dying to self and living unto God. This is not to imply that unbelievers are unable to form a good and lasting marriage. But whenever a marriage functions as it should, it is because the principles of God (whether acknowledged or not) are incorporated into that marriage.

The Natural Ways of Male and Female

In the creative order, the male is the initiator and the female the responder. This, of course, is not an absolute, but a general principle. Obviously, the "woman of valor" in Proverbs 31 does plenty of initiating! And a man who has learned humility also has learned to respond to the needs of others. But in the broad scope of things, men initiate, and women respond. Now it can be seen that the scenario suggested above, in the interpretation of Genesis 3:16, has these roles reversed. The woman, needing the security of her husband in the face of promised pain, initiates a way to control her husband. This is because she fears (and with good reason) that her husband does not have her interests as a top priority. Conversely, because the man has become self-centered, he does not initiate the measures necessary to offer the security his wife needs. Thus, he only responds to her attempts at controlling him.

This reality is found in the caricatures often heard regarding men and women. The man is characterized as "doing his own thing," and not really taking the initiative to "get things done" that need to be done. After a hard day's work, he is content to entertain himself, or spend time with guys. Conversely, woman is caricatured as scheming to get her man to do the necessary things. Learning the fine art of "controlling," the woman uses everything at her disposal to get her man to meet her needs: she nags, applies guilt, uses the "silent treatment," becomes alluring, bribes, etc. None of this works long-term, however. The more she tries to control, the more he resists. And the more he resists, the more she tries to control. The whole pattern spirals until one or the other gives up, communication stops, and the relationship falls on hard times, or fails all together.

Isn't it interesting that the commands given to husbands and wives in the Apostolic Scriptures speak directly to this very issue? The command to husbands is: "love your wives as Messiah loved His congregation" (Ephesians 5:25). That means self-sacrificing love, the kind that puts one's own desires and needs as secondary to those of one's wife. And to the wives the command is given: "be subject to your husbands" (Colossians 3:18, cf. Ephesians 5:22, 24). To the man whose natural tendency will be to fulfill his own needs and neglect those of his wife, the Scriptures enjoin humble service—a dying to oneself—a willingness to initiate whatever is needed to provide the security and companionship that she so much needs and desires. To the woman whose need for security produces her penchant to control her husband, the Scriptures enjoin submission to him, a submission that projects trust and loyalty.

Surely this highlights the fact that God's ways are not our ways! Because we discover that when we follow God's commands, we actually receive what we thought we could only achieve by our fallen methods. A man who dies to his own desires, and puts his wife's needs above his own, will discover that his wife is the companion he had always longed for, and that she provides a strength for him that can be found nowhere else. And the submissive wife discovers that her husband takes the initiative, responds to her needs, and provides the security she thought was available only if she controlled him.

What is more, when husbands and wives submit to God's pattern for marriage, the result is shalom—shalom in one's soul, shalom in one's home, and a shalom that fosters enduring family righteousness.

But the key is trusting God. Do we believe that God is good, or are we giving into the lie of the Deceiver, that perhaps God's ways don't always work—that God is, at times, not entirely good? Accepting God's way for marriage is not natural for us. It goes against our sinful nature and it runs rough-shod over the patterns of human society. Women often think that submitting to a man who has not shown humility will only cause them more pain. And men give way to the notion that putting their wife's needs before their own will only allow her to take advantage of his kindness. But do we trust God? Do we believe that, though His ways are contrary to our natural way of thinking, they are, nonetheless, the right ways, and ways that work?

So here is the heart of the matter: trusting God is the way to success in our relationships and marriages. It all comes back to a matter of faith! Even as Adam and Chavah first broke with God, and then with each other, so the way back is a restored trust in the goodness of God, and a willingness to venture out upon His goodness.

Let's Summarize

1. One of Satan's schemes for hiding the image of God in mankind is to cause division between a husband and wife.

2. Satan's first attack was against God. He suggested that God actually was not good and could not be trusted.

3. When Adam and Chavah disobeyed God, they were asserting their independence from God.

4. In Genesis 3:16, and the phrase "your desire will be for your husband," the word "desire" means "to dominate."

5. In Genesis 3:16, and the phrase "but he will rule over you," to "rule over" means "to subdue."

6. A woman naturally thinks that controlling her husband will give her security.

7. A man's natural tendency to self-centeredness will cause him to neglect his wife's needs.

8. The Scriptures enjoin men to love their wives, and for wives to submit to their husbands.

9. The bottom-line issue is whether we trust God and are willing to follow His guidelines for marriage relationships.

Talk About It!

1. If men are suppose to be leaders, why do they often have difficulty taking the initiative?

2. What is "nagging" and why do men resist it?

3. How does a young woman learn the art of submission? How does a

young man learn the art of leading?

4. Why does one's relationship with God directly affect one's relationship with one's spouse?

Chapter 3
Marriage as a Covenant

In our times, the definition of marriage has come into question: what exactly constitutes "marriage?" When is a marriage legitimate, and when is it not? And furthermore, is marriage even necessary?

The moral decline of our society and world has even questioned whether a legitimate marriage can exist between people of the same sex, so it is no wonder that the traditional views of marriage are all considered out dated and irrelevant for our modern world. In reality, the question has become one of whether marriage is even necessary. Wouldn't it be just as acceptable for two committed individuals to form a private agreement together regarding their relationship? Who needs the recognition of others? "If it's right for us, that should be enough!"

In the face of these questions, we are driven back to our foundations, namely, that we believe God is the Creator, and as such, He has the right and authority to prescribe the manner in which He desires His creation to function. Or to put it simply: God is both the Creator and the Law-giver. So the more fundamental question that we always face is this: are we willing to accept God and His revelation of truth as the basis for how we live our lives, or do we believe that we can exist independent of Him and make up our own minds about what is right and wrong?

Obviously, mankind made the decision from the very beginning to live independently of God—to disregard His commandments in favor of satisfying their own desires. And so it is not surprising that the basic tendency of humankind has always been to seek our own way, and to disregard the ways of God—we inherited this from Adam and Chavah. This tendency is nowhere more often seen than in the whole matter of marriage. And this, likewise, should not be a surprise. If, as we have noted above, the union of man and wife in marriage offers one of the most strategic ways in which the very image of God is seen, then we should expect that the enemy would do everything possible to destroy marriages. And one of the craftiest ways that Satan has sought to destroy marriage is to lead mankind to redefine it, or to even consider it unnecessary or irrelevant.

Those of us who believe that God is, and that He is the One who rewards those who seek Him (Heb 11:6), rely upon the word of God (the Bible) to teach us what God thinks of marriage, how He defines it, and what He expects of us in the realm of marriage. Once again, we come back to the eternal words of our King as the basis for what we know to be true, and how we live out this truth.

Genesis 2:24

> For this reason a man shall leave his father and his mother, and be joined to his wife; and they shall become one flesh.

עַל־כֵּן יַעֲזָב־אִישׁ אֶת־אָבִיו וְאֶת־אִמּוֹ וְדָבַק בְּאִשְׁתּוֹ וְהָיוּ לְבָשָׂר אֶחָד

In Matthew 19, we see some Pharisees approaching our Master, testing Him with regard to the whole issue of marriage. It is likely that these Pharisees followed the teaching of Hillel, who was very liberal on the matter of divorce. According to Hillel's teaching, a man could divorce his wife for any number of things. Hillel's rival in the Sanhedrin of that day was Shammai, whose teaching on marriage and divorce was far more restrictive. Shammai taught that divorce was only lawful when there was clear, sexual infidelity within the marriage. It seems apparent that Yeshua agreed with Shammai against Hillel, and this brought up the debate recorded in Matthew 19. The Pharisees were testing Yeshua regarding His strong position on marriage, and His very restrictive view regarding the legitimacy of divorce.

The Pharisees open with this question: "Is it lawful for a man to divorce his wife for any reason at all?" In other words, "Do you agree that Hillel is right in offering any number of reason for a man to legitimately divorce his wife?" As is often the case, our Master "cuts to the bottom-line." Rather than engage in *halachic* debate over divorce, Yeshua immediately goes to the very foundation of marriage itself, and in so doing, He bases His teaching on Genesis 2:24.

> Matt 19:4 And He answered and said, "Have you not read that He who created them from the beginning made them male and female, 5 and said, 'For this reason a man shall leave his father and mother and be joined to

his wife, and the two shall become one flesh'? 6 "So they are no longer two, but one flesh. What therefore God has joined together, let no man separate."

This in itself should teach us that the inspired words of Moses in Genesis 2:24 form a sure foundation for what marriage is, and how it functions in the life of a man and woman.

There are a number of important things we should glean from a closer look at Genesis 2:24, and Yeshua's use of it in His own teaching on marriage. First, note that He begins by affirming that God created male and female from the beginning. Why does He begin by stating that? Surely the Pharisees agreed that God created male and female from the beginning! But the reason that our Master begins by stating this obvious fact is to emphasize that the ability of male and female to become one is the basis for Moses' statement. That God created male and female forms the basis for Moses' words "For this reason ...." Because God created mankind in the diversity of male and female, and because God intends that the union of male and female portray His own oneness, He instituted marriage as the means by which mankind would be able to reflect His very image.

Secondly, we note that the union between a man and a woman involves two phases: 1) the man *leaves* his father and mother, and 2) he is *joined* to his wife. Thus, in order for marriage to be as God intends it, both of these must occur.

What does it mean for a man to *leave* his father and mother? First, we know that this does not mean to "forsake" in the sense of dishonoring one's parents. The Torah specifically calls upon children to honor their parents, and the Sages are right on the mark when they teach that such honor is best seen when children care for their aged parents. Yeshua agrees with this when He reprimands some in His day who were trying to appear pious by donating their wealth to the Temple for a period of time in order to keep from giving it to their aged parents (Mark 7:10–12). So *leaving* father and mother cannot be in conflict with honoring them. When a man is ready for marriage, he must *leave* father and mother, but he must do so in a way that honors them. This in itself tells us that *his parents are part of the whole decision for him to marry in the first place.* Leaving father and mother is therefore not a unilateral decision—a decision the young man makes on his own. It is rather a decision that includes his parents as well.

Granted, we are talking about the ideal here. Not every young man has a living mother and father. Moreover, in the break up families, a young man may have little or no relationship with his mother or with his father. But we are seeking to implement the ideal—we're not trying to define and implement marriage according to the brokenness of our sinful world. Surely, in those situations where a young man grows up in a broken family, he will have to do the best he can to honor parents (even when they've been dishonorable), and to fulfill the duty of *leaving* in a righteous way.

So the command to *leave* father and mother cuts two directions: it is a requirement of the young man, but it is also a strong directive to parents, that they maintain their own marriage, and their role as father and mother, in order to facilitate this *leaving* process as a young man anticipates marriage.

But what does *leaving* mean then? The Hebrew word is עָזַב, *'azav,* and can mean "to leave," but also "to abandon," "give up," or "to let go." The word obviously speaks of a change in relationship. *'azav* pictures turning away from something one previously faced. The picture is quite simple: from his youth, a boy depends upon his father and mother for food, protection, love, and guidance. Moreover, the parents are obligated to provide these for their son. The growing boy has a relationship of dependence upon his parents, and the parents have the authority and obligation to care for him in all areas of his life. But when the young man *leaves* his father and mother, he accepts the responsibility of providing for himself and his wife. Surely the child/parent relationship continues, and the love and friendship fostered during his years of growing up also continues. But in *leaving,* the young man has committed himself to forming his own home, and providing for himself through his own work. He takes on a new relationship with his parents, one which is still characterized by honoring them, but one that establishes an authority directly under God, and not primarily through his parents. In short, by *leaving* his father and mother, he accepts the responsibilities of establishing a new home.

Hopefully, he has been trained during his years at home for this awesome responsibility. As he became of age, and went through the tradition of becoming a *bar mitzvah*,[1] he began to recognize that he had a direct responsibility to God, and that there would come a day when he would be on his own, and would need to establish a home where God's authority was lived out through his personal obedience—a home where his children would begin the cycle all over again.

Thus, *leaving* father and mother in this context describes a change in the authority structure, and an acceptance of the responsibilities to be a provider and leader in a newly established home.

It is important to note that the man is to *leave* both father and mother. Most often, the father/son relationship is one mark primarily by authority: the father ought to be the head of the family, and thus it is the father who most often projects the figure of authority within the family. Surely this should not negate a relationship of warmth and friendship! Authority apart from genuine love rings hallow. But when a young man *leaves* his father, he recognizes that he is now directly responsible to God apart from the role his father played as his immediate authority.

Leaving mother is another matter all together. The mother most often supplies the role of nurturer. From the beginning she nursed and cared for her son, and continued through his growing years to offer to him a taste of the male/female relationship marked by hugs and motherly protection. As the son *leaves* his mother, he also *leaves* that place of being nurtured by her. He will have to find that warmth of feminine nurture, which a man always needs, in his wife.

While Genesis 2:24 describes the need for a young man to *leave* father and mother, we can also see that Godly parents will take an active role in helping him do that. Fathers that continue to approach their sons as a primary authority figure, will hamper the young man from standing on his own two feet, and accepting the responsibility of his own home. Likewise, mothers who seek to be a primary nurturer to their son after he leaves will get in the way of the second command in our text, the command for the son to be *joined* to his wife. The role of parents after a son

1   Regardless of whether a young boy goes through the ritual of bar mitzvah or not, there should come a time in his life where parents let him know that he has gained new levels of responsibility, both to his fellowman as well as to God. It is unfortunate that in our modern society, parents neglect the importance of this. It is not unusual to see young men who never are required to accept personal responsibilities until they are 18 or older. That's probably too late. Young boys need to realize that as they grow older, they will be expected to take on more and more personal responsibilities, because this will help prepare them for the time when they will leave father and mother and carry the full responsibilities of a man in the community.

leaves and is joined to his wife, is primarily that of counsellors and en-couragers.

It is also instructive, as we consider what *leaving* means in our text, that the command is directed to the man and not to the woman. We will consider this in more detail when we discuss the issue of betrothal, but it is apparent in this foundational text that a daughter remains under the authority and protection of her parents until such time as she is mar-ried, and thus comes under the shelter of her husband.

The second part of our verse (Genesis 2:24) instructs the man to be *joined* to his wife. As we have seen, *leaving* father and mother is neces-sary in order for him to be *joined* to his wife. The word translated *joined* is דָּבַק, *dabaq,* "to stick to," "to cling, cleave to." This word is used of one's relationship to God:

> Deut. 10:20 "You shall fear the Lord your God; you shall serve Him and cling to Him, and you shall swear by His name.

> Deut. 11:22 "For if you are careful to keep all this commandment which I am commanding you to do, to love the Lord your God, to walk in all His ways and hold fast to Him ..."

It is important for us to focus on this word *dabaq,* because it is here that we get the first glimpse of marriage as a covenant. The use of this word in the above instances is within the covenant setting of Deuteronomy. Israel, as the covenant partner with God, is instructed to *cling* to Him. This is surrounded by commandments to obey Him, to walk in His ways, to fear Him, to serve Him, and to swear by His name. Thus, the word *dabaq* em-phasizes the need for Israel to maintain her covenant partnership with God as an exclusive relationship. In clinging to Him, she would be unable to attach herself to any other god, or to put it another way, Israel would not enter into covenant relationship with pagan deities.

What exactly is a "covenant?" There has been much written on this, mostly dealing with the meaning of the word בְּרִית, *berit.* But for our purposes here, we may simply say that a covenant is "an elected, as opposed to a natural, relationship of obligation under oath."[2] What this definition entails is: 1) a covenant establishes a relationship, 2) this re-lationship is one of choice, not of bloodline, 3) a covenant establishes obligations, and 4) these obligations are given weight by taking an oath.

2.   Quoted from Gordon P. Hugenberger, *Marriage as a Covenant* (Baker, 1994), p. 11.

If we use this working definition of "covenant," we can see that the parent/child relationship is not a covenant. It occurs naturally through the process of birth. However, the husband/wife relationship, as pictured in seed form in Genesis 2:24, appears very much as a covenant relationship. The man leaves the natural relationship of his parents, and is *joined* to his wife, meaning he has taken upon himself a unique relationship with his wife, designated as being *joined* to her. In the same manner in which Israel is commanded to be *joined* to God in covenant relationship, Moses, using the same word, gives us a strong hint that the male/female relationship of marriage is also cast in covenant terms, describing a unique and exclusive relationship entered into by choice, not as the result of nature.

Thus, the idea inherent in the word *dabaq* is first one of covenant relationship. A relationship built upon a personal choice, and which is characterized by an enduring exclusivity. For the man to *cling* to his wife means he has forsaken others in favor of her, and he has committed himself to this relationship in a covenant sense.

Granted, Genesis 2:24 does not spell this out explicitly. The on-going revelation of the Tanach and of the Apostolic Scriptures will make this description of marriage as a covenant far more explicit. But from the beginning, Moses uses terms in connection with marriage that clearly points us in this direction.

But the word Moses uses, *dabaq*, "to join to" or "to cling to" goes beyond the hinting of covenant relationship as merely a legal or binding covenant. It casts this relationship in terms most intimate and personal. *Dabaq* envisions an intertwining of lives to such an extent that they cannot be severed.

The closest practical idea we can derive from this is that of physical attachment—hugging, and the intimate sexual relationship that comes between a husband and his wife. This is the physical or outward manifestation of the inward or heart commitment of the covenant. And thus, Moses concludes this foundational verse with the phrase, "and they shall become one flesh" (literally, "and they shall be for flesh, one"). He puts the word "one" last in order to emphasize it. With regard to their earthly existence, the husband and wife have so joined themselves together that their lives are now envisioned as one and the same.

This idea of marriage as covenant is further strengthened by our own Master's commentary on our verse. After quoting Genesis 2:24 as His primary text, He concludes:

Matt 19:6 "So they are no longer two, but one flesh. What therefore God
has joined together, let no man separate."

He emphasizes the oneness principle, and then states that it is God that
has joined them together. In other words, even though the covenant of
marriage is an elective one between a man and his wife, their ability to be
joined as one flesh is the work of God, for He created male and female for
this purpose, and with this ability.

The words of our Master have great significance for our understanding of marriage as a covenant. The joining or covenant aspect of
marriage is not merely entered into by the couple themselves, but God
stands as part of the covenant transaction. He is the One Who joins them,
Who gives sanctity and value to the covenant of marriage. In every Godly
marriage, then, there is a partnership not just between the husband and
wife, but with God as well. God is the eternal "match-maker." He is the
One Who, from the beginning, created male and female with the ability to
become one, and He is the One Who, in His gracious providence, works
out all of the necessary details to bring a man and woman together.

The Sages speak of this in the Talmud (b.*Sota* 2a):

Forty days before conception it is decreed in heaven: "The daughter of
this person is for the son of that person!"

Indeed, if we believe that all things are ordained by God, then surely we
must believe that our marriages are also so ordained. I know, of course,
that some would question this because they have entered into marriages
that have failed, or that were "wrong from the beginning," and so forth.
But we dare not make the rule on the basis of the exceptions. Furthermore,
how we understand this principle will affect our decisions when things are
not so good within a marriage. Believing that God has ordained the person
I have married to be my spouse, will be a strong incentive to maintain the
covenant that has Him as a partner.

Think about it for a minute! If we honestly believe that our loving
Father in heaven has carefully chosen the one with whom we will spend
the majority of our days upon this earth, then this empowers us to look at
our spouse as God's chosen gift to us. We are two parts of a whole that
God has joined together. That was His doing, and that means that He also
will give us the strength and ability to remain together through good and

bad. That is because "finding each other" is only the beginning of the story, not the key to success. Actually, "finding each other" is a life-long process, in which we continue to discover in each other one's "other half." This takes discipline, self-sacrifice, and sometimes plain hard work! But in committing ourselves to marriage as a life-long covenant, we begin on the right path. We give ourselves to what we know God has already done.

This principle, that God is the One Who joins a man to his wife, is best demonstrated in the example of Adam and Chavah. God fashions Chavah from a rib of Adam, and then presents her to him. God has made the choice, worked out all of the details, and created a oneness between man and wife. Adam never wondered if he had chosen the right woman—there were no others! Likewise, Chavah knew that she had been given Adam as her chosen beloved. He was the only man around!

I'm sure that some single adults wish their situation could be that easy. If there were only one choice, the choice would be obvious. But in reality, there *is* only one choice, and that is the one God has chosen for each of us who are to be married. Trusting Him in that decision, and believing Him after the decision is made, will make all the difference in the world when it comes to commitment in marriage.

In summary, then, the first, and thus foundational, text of the Torah that deals with the marriage relationship is Genesis 2:24. In this verse we learn that 1) a man *leaves* his father and mother, meaning that there is a change of authority and responsibility, 2) that he is *joined* to his wife, meaning that he establishes a covenant relationship with his wife, one which includes God as a covenant partner, and 3) that this covenant between husband and wife is something ordained by God Himself, worked out in time through His mysterious providence.

Let's Talk About It!

1. Summarize what is meant by a man *leaving* his father and mother.
   Why is it that many sons are ready to leave home as they approach
   adulthood?

2. What can parents do to help prepare a son for *leaving* as Gen 2:24
   commands? What can parents do to hinder this?

3. Describe how the use of the word "to cling" in Deut 10:20 and
   11:22 may help us understand the same word in Gen 2:24. (You
   might want to look this word up in a concordance to find other passages to compare as well.)

4. If we believe that God has chosen the one we are to marry, how
   will this make a difference when we encounter troubles in our marriage relationship?

5. Consider this scenario: A newly married couple invites the husband's parents over for dinner. While his wife is busy finishing
   things in the kitchen, her mother-in-law rearranges some pictures
   on the living room wall, because she thinks they were not placed
   properly. When the young wife sees what her mother-in-law has
   done, she is quite upset!

   a) how could this problem have been avoided?
   b) what should be the first thing the newly married wife does?
   c) what should the role of the newly married husband be in this
   situation?

6. We have begun to see that marriage is presented in the Bible as a
   covenant. Why does this make it all that much more important to
   be careful about entering into marriage?

Chapter 4
Marriage as a Covenant, Part 2

In the previous chapter we saw how marriage as a covenant is first based upon Genesis 2:24, "For this reason a man shall leave his father and his mother, and be joined to his wife; and they shall become one flesh." While this text does not specifically denote the relationship between male and female as a covenant, it gives in seed form the elements of a covenant. Specifically, we learned that this involved *leaving* the natural relationship of son to father and mother, and *joining* his wife. This joining involves a commitment to a relationship that is not the result of biological relationship, but one of choice. Moreover, the idea of *joining* pictures intimate joining of two lives to form an unbreakable union—"they shall become one flesh." We therefore took this simple definition of "covenant" as it pertains to marriage: the marriage covenant is an "elected, as opposed to a natural, relationship of obligation under oath."

There are other Scriptures that consider the bond of marriage as covenant. For instance, in Proverbs 2, the father implores his sons to receive his instruction, and to seek after wisdom. In doing so, he will guard his steps from the paths of unrighteousness, and live his life (walk) in the ways of truth and uprightness. Wisdom will be a safeguard against the ways of the one who speaks perverseness (v. 12), from those who walk in the paths of darkness (v. 13), those who love evil and rejoice in wickedness (v. 14). This wisdom will also keep the son from being enticed by the "strange woman," who would seek to entice a man into sexual sins. Note how the Proverbs describe such a woman (vv. 16–19):

> To deliver you from the strange woman, From the adulteress who flatters with her words; That leaves the companion of her youth And forgets the covenant of her God; For her house sinks down to death And her tracks lead to the dead; None who go to her return again, Nor do they reach the paths of life.

The adulterous woman is characterized as leaving the companion of her youth, that is, her husband whom she married as a young woman. But in so doing, she "forgets the covenant of her God." Some commentators and scholars have understood this to mean the general covenant of the Torah in which she was raised. And this could, of course, be a possible meaning. But in the poetic parallelism of this verse, "forgetting the covenant of her God" is parallel to "leaving the companion of her youth." I think it more likely that here the marriage union is considered to be a covenant, not only between the husband and wife, but also between husband and wife and God. As Yeshua instructed us in His commentary on Genesis 2:24, "what God has joined together, let no man separate" (Matthew 19:6). God is the One Who does the joining, and He does this not only by providentially bringing together those He has designed to be married, but also by being the divine witness to their covenant together. When a husband or wife forgets the covenant he or she has made in the marriage union, it is not merely a breach of trust between the two of them, but also in relationship to God Who did the joining in the first place, and remains a witness to the covenant of marriage.

We should note several important things from this description in Proverbs 2. First, a man needs to be guarded from the paths of unrighteousness, and in this case, particularly from the ways of the strange woman. This should teach us that a man, in his flesh, is susceptible to being trapped by the ways of a strange woman. It is foolish to think that only some men, those with perverted minds, are drawn to sexual sin. Any man, if he leaves himself unguarded, can be drawn away by his own lusts to the sins of immorality. This is the point of Solomon's instructions here: wisdom, that is, viewing life from God's perspective, and accepting His ways as right and good, will be a safeguard against a man's own natural inclinations. Our present society has been overrun with immorality, and there is opportunity for engaging in sexual sins at every turn. If a man intends to enter into a lasting, covenant relationship of marriage, he must begin at an early age to discipline himself in the ways of godliness and wisdom. He must make it a set pattern of his life that he formulates his decisions, whether small or large, upon the righteous ways of God. And he can never think for a moment that he has "arrived" at a place where he no longer needs such discipline in righteousness. As men we must always reckon with the fact that only God's wisdom can form a sure defense against the weakness of our own flesh, and the constant drone of the world that calls us to engage in her wicked ways.

Thus, the spiritual health of a man—his personal relationship with God and his disciplined life of spiritual growth, is an essential quality necessary for being a good husband. Young ladies and their parents who are looking for a future husband do well, then, to consider this as a most important priority. Whereas the world will mock a young man for putting spiritual things first, in reality, such a characteristic ought to be one of the most important criteria when looking for a husband. A young man who has not learned to put God first in his life may well be susceptible to things that would destroy a marriage.

Secondly, note that Proverbs 2:16 describes the strange woman as one who "flatters with her words." The word "flatters" (חֶלִיקָה, *chelikah*) is based upon the root meaning "smooth." Her words are smooth, meaning that she says things that appeal and are easy to receive. If we keep in mind the general disposition of male and female following the entrance of sin into the world, we remember that a woman's greatest need is to find security in her world—a way to deal with the pain that life would inevitably bring her way. The man, as the one who should provide such security, faces the constant threat of failure in his duties. As provider and protector, his abilities are constantly tested and he daily faces the question of whether or not he will be able to perform the tasks required of him. It is not unusual to find men who, because of the fear of failure, are afraid to venture out into the unknown. Looking for a new job, for instance, is often a far bigger trauma to a man than most women realize. Granted, no one likes being rejected! But for a man to be told he does not qualify for a job (for instance) hits at the very core of his manliness. Men therefore have a tendency to overcome such fear by boasting of their abilities, and the "male ego" results from a deep-seated fear of failure.

This makes "smooth words" very effective. When the strange woman builds up a man with flattery, it draws him in because it feeds his self-confidence. This is all the more true if, in his own marriage, he rarely receives from his wife words of encouragement and thankfulness for what he does in providing and protecting. On the other hand, when a wife nurtures her husband by letting him know, both in word and deed, that she finds in him a man who is successful in his duties as a man, it strengthens his resolve to continue to work hard to fulfill his role.

But the man who is growing spiritually before the Lord, will first find his commendations from the Almighty Himself, and particularly from the Scriptures that are the words of God. Here, in the unchanging and eternal words of the Creator, a man led by the Spirit will find his true strength, not in his own abilities, but in the strength that comes from reliance upon God. Admitting his weakness before the Lord will put him in a place of trust and therefore a place of strength. And it will be his desire to honor God in the covenant of marriage, first and foremost, that will give him the strength to maintain faithfulness even in difficult times.

Thirdly, the wayward woman leaves the companion of her youth—the husband with whom she first entered the marriage covenant. She has proven herself unwilling to maintain the covenant of marriage, yet she presents herself as one who understands and is able to fulfill the needs of another man. How foolish for man to think that such a woman really has his needs as her priority! If she were one who could honestly meet his needs, she would be doing that for her husband. Her approach is therefore one of deception, and is in fact a trap which, as our text indicates, snares the foolish man, and takes his life.

If, as I have noted above, one of the priorities in looking for a husband is to find a man who is intent on growing spiritually in his faith before God, then it is equally true that a top priority when looking for a wife is the same. A young woman who has proven herself able to remain submissive to the authority of her parents, as an act of obedience before God, has learned a very significant lesson for life. Her determination to live obediently within God's commandments, to put her faith in Yeshua as the top duty and joy of her life, is a woman who will do the same in the covenant of marriage. As she faithfully strives to please the Almighty in maintaining her covenant oath before Him, she will receive the strength to be the wife He intends her to be.

Another passage that speaks of marriage as a covenant is Malachai 2. Here, the prophet is chastising Israel for her sinful ways. In the first 12 verses, the prophet speaks to the priests, those of the tribe of Levi. They have neglected God's specific instructions in terms of their priestly duties, most likely adding aspects of pagan worship into their sacred duties ("married the daughter of a foreign god," v. 11). In v. 13ff, the prophet turns to the issue of marriage and divorce. He writes:

> "This is another thing you do: you cover the altar of the Lord with tears, with weeping and with groaning, because He no longer regards the offering or accepts it with favor from your hand. Yet you say, 'For what reason?' Because the Lord has been a witness between you and the wife of your youth, against whom you have dealt treacherously, though she is your companion and your wife by covenant."

Again, while some commentators try to construe the phrase "wife by covenant" as speaking to Israel as God's covenant partner, the context surely favors understanding the phrase as pertaining to the marriage between a man and woman. Here the text specifically labels marriage as a covenant, made between a husband and wife, with God as the witness. Whether this is addressed specifically to the priests, or to the nation as a whole, the point is still clear: in breaking the covenant of marriage through divorce, God has withdrawn His blessing from Israel, for He does not accept the sacrifices that have been offered by those whose hearts have willfully disregarded His ways in marriage. Interestingly, in perhaps a parallel to this, Peter suggests that if a husband fails to show honor to his wife as one who is a fellow-partaker in God's grace, it may result in their prayers "being hindered" (1Pet 3:7). The point is simply that if a husband and wife are not willing to treat each other in the manner consistent with the covenant of marriage, they should not expect that God would heed their prayers. "If I regard iniquity in my heart, the Lord will not hear *me*" (Ps 66:18).

It is clear, then, that the Tanach presents marriage as a covenant between a man, and woman, and God. But what does this mean in terms of how a marriage should be recognized or entered into? First, as I have already noted, a covenant is a relationship by choice, not by nature. This means that marriage as God intends it is not something that can be forced upon anyone. The common practice in the Ancient world, and which still obtains in some parts of our modern world, that monarchs would marry for political reasons, finds no basis in God's description of marriage. Secondly, the role of the parents in protecting the daughter, and in procuring a husband for her, must always take into full consideration the daughter's own decision. While the parents play a key role in protecting and providing for their daughter when it comes to finding her a husband, the covenant of marriage into which she will enter is one that she must make. If the whole matter of courting is to be successful, it must always be with the full and willing consent of their daughter. Anything less is a recipe for disaster.

Another important practical ramification of marriage as a covenant is that it includes an oath. If we study covenants in general as found in the Scriptures, we discover that one consistent element of a covenant relationship is the taking of an oath that binds the covenant partners. In the covenant made with Abraham, for instance, God is the One Who takes the oath, as symbolized by the smoking pot and flaming torch that passed between the slain parts of the sacrificial animals (Gen 15). In essence, what this acted-out covenant ceremony said was, "May I become like these if I do not fulfill the covenant." God pledged His own life when He made the covenant with Abraham (cf. Gen 22:16). The author of Hebrews speaks to this when he writes (Heb 6:13):

> For when God made the promise to Abraham, since He could swear by no one greater, He swore by Himself...

God likewise takes the covenant oath in the covenant with David (Ps 89:35–37):

> "Once I have sworn by My holiness; I will not lie to David. His descendants shall endure forever and his throne as the sun before Me. It shall be established forever like the moon, and the witness in the sky is faithful."

Likewise, the covenant between Abraham and Abimelech involved an oath (Gen 21:31), as did the covenant between Isaac's servants and the herdsmen of the Philistines (Gen 26:28ff). Indeed, the idea of an "oath" as part and parcel with covenant in the biblical world is seen in that it is used at times as synonymous with "covenant" (Psa. 105:9; Ezek. 16:59; 17:16; Luke 1:73).

Now a covenant oath is valid only when there are witnesses to the oath. For in the case where an oath exists only between two parties, there is no solid proof that the oath was ever taken: it is the word of one against the other. Yet the Torah teaches that only in the mouth of two or three is a matter established. In the case where two might take an oath without witness, each one has only himself or herself as a witness. It is for this reason that a valid oath requires multiple witnesses.

What does this mean for the covenant of marriage? *It means that the covenant of marriage involves more than just the man and woman who are entering into marriage.* Thus, the covenant of marriage must be witnessed by others in order for it to be valid. This is of particular importance in our times, when the idea has grown in popularity that a man and a woman who make a pact between themselves is sufficient to establish a biblical marriage. Such a view discounts the necessity and value of an oath.

The Sages determined that a valid marriage oath must be witnessed by at least two witnesses. While this is strictly rabbinic, it nonetheless was an attempt to honor the pattern of marriage found in the Scriptures in which marriage was seen as a covenant which required a valid oath, which in turn required multiple witnesses. This Hebraic custom set the pattern for marriage wherever the Judeo-Christian ethic obtained, and is still in force in our own times. For instance, a marriage license in our own country has a requirement for two witnesses besides the bride and the groom.

The important aspect that this brings to our discussion of marriage as covenant is that marriage is always viewed in the Bible as involving the wider community. This negates the idea that a couple who decide to live together as husband and wife are, in God's eyes, married. Living together as husband and wife, without the public enactment of the covenant of marriage, constitutes fornication, not marriage. In fact, it is precisely the public marriage ceremony that marks the distinction between illicit relationships and marriage as honored by God.

At first blush, this may seem arbitrary. If a man and woman love each other, and have covenanted together to be joined in marriage, isn't that enough? Why must their marriage covenant be enacted with a public oath? The answer has both a practical as well as a scriptural dimension. Practically, the public oath of marriage gives strength to the covenant of marriage. When a couple enters into the covenant marriage by taking a public oath, the witnesses who observe their oath to each other stand ready to make sure the couple maintains their oath. When their relationship comes into difficulties, the community is there both to hold them to their word as well as to encourage and help them to maintain their marriage covenant. But there is also a spiritual dimension to the public marriage oath: marriage is, in its ultimate sense, a picture of the relationship between God and His people, and specifically between Yeshua and His congregation (Eph 5:32). As the community gathers to witness the marriage ceremony, they see acted out before them the very covenant of which each one is a member: the covenant of marriage between the Almighty and His chosen bride. Without the public aspect of the oath in the marriage covenant, this most important function of marriage is diminished.

We see, then, that viewing marriage as a covenant actually involves four parties: the bride, the groom, God, and the community. By community I mean those family members and friends who have a mutual commitment to each other, including the bride and the groom.

This brings up the question of the role of the government in marriage. Do the Scriptures require that a bride and groom have their marriage recognized by the government of the land in which they reside? The answer is "no." Nothing in the Bible indicates that such is a necessity. It does not forbid it, but neither does it require it. In fact, there have been times throughout history when a godless government forbade marriage as prescribed by God's word. For instance, in places where anti-Semitism prevailed, Jewish people have been forbidden to marry. But the Scriptures never require the government's "okay" in order to enter into a valid marriage.

In our own country, however, while obtaining a government issued marriage license is surely not required by God, it should be considered within the realm of wisdom. Since obtaining such a license in no way (at least currently) requires any compromise of biblical mandates, it seems wise to do so. This is primarily because recognition by the government of one's marriage has legal ramifications in terms of property ownership and inheritance. If a couple were to be validly married but did not register their marriage with the local government, it would be far more difficult for either the husband or the wife to legally retain ownership of property in the event of a death.[1] Moreover, as long as registration of marriages with the government in no way compromises the biblical pattern of marriage, to do so honors the general Scriptural mandate to practice submission to those in authority.

In summary, then, marriage as a covenant teaches the following:

1. The relationship of marriage is something that is a binding relationship. As a covenant, it cannot be broken at will.

2. The relationship of marriage is one of choice, it cannot be forced upon anyone.

3. The relationship of marriage as covenant is between husband, wife, and God, as witnessed by others (community).

4. The relationship of marriage as covenant is based upon an oath taken between the husband and wife, witnessed by God and other

---

1   It is not clear what authorities Paul identifies in Romans 13:1f. Traditionally these have been viewed as "government" authorities (so the NASB), but it may be that Paul is referring to synagogue authorities. Regardless, the words of our Master regarding the paying of taxes (Matt 22:21) gives us an example of how we should act. When submission to government authorities does not in any way violate our obedience to God, we should submit to their rule.

witnesses (the community). As such, it is a covenant that must be maintained and cannot be considered temporary.

5. Since taking an oath before God and with God as a covenant member is a very serious matter, the relationship of marriage must be entered with due appreciation for what the covenant of marriage entails.

6. The public aspect of the marriage ceremony (oath taking) fulfills both the practical aspect of the oath (giving it strength as it is witnessed by others) and the spiritual value, in that it reminds the community of the marriage covenant between God and His chosen people.

Let's Talk About It!

1. In what practical ways is a man's discipline in spiritual growth directly related to his being guarded from sexual sin?

2. Why are men sometimes "drawn" into a possible bad situation by flattery? How can you tell the difference between "flattery" and genuine compliments?

3. What practical things can a young man do to prepare himself to be a faithful covenant partner? What are some characteristics of a young man that would indicate he would be able to remain faithful in a covenant situation?

4. What practical things can a young woman do to prepare herself to be a faithful covenant partner? What are the characteristics of a young woman that would indicate she would be able to remain faithful in a covenant situation?

5. What are some practical ways that a wife can express to her husband that she appreciates his efforts to provide for and protect her? (Don't overlook the obvious!)

6. Why is it necessary for a marriage ceremony to be public?

7. What are the consequences of taking an oath? What are the consequences of breaking an oath?

8. Discuss how the relationship between a husband and his wife should portray the relationship between Yeshua and His congregation.

Chapter 5
Characteristics of a Godly Husband

When we seek to know what the Torah teaches us about the role of a husband, we may begin with the notice of Genesis 2:24, which we have already studied, that "they shall be one flesh" (וְהָיוּ לְבָשָׂר אֶחָד).

A story is told of a *tzaddik* of Jerusalem, Rabbi Aryeh Levin. He accompanied his wife to the doctor one day, and when the physician asked what was the matter, R. Aryeh answered, "My wife's foot hurts us." R. Aryeh understood the power of the word "us" in the marriage relationship, and was living out the reality of "they shall be one flesh." The pain his wife was suffering had become his own pain.

Paul has this same idea in mind when he writes in Eph 5:28–29:

> So husbands ought also to love their own wives as their own bodies. He who loves his own wife loves himself; for no one ever hated his own flesh, but nourishes and cherishes it, just as Messiah also does His *kehilah* ...

The goal, then, for a man who desires to be a Godly husband, is to align his own personality and nature with his wife's, and to forge together their lives in such a way so as to fulfill the *mitzvah* of being one flesh.

Thus, the Torah's expectations for marriage are very high. The marriage relationship is not one of simply co-existing, or of "putting up" with each other, but of losing one's own life in order to unite with the life of one's spouse. We see that for Paul, the ultimate example of this is to be found in the Messiah Himself: "Husbands, love your wives, just as Messiah also loved His *kehilah* and gave Himself up for her" (Eph 5:25).

This is not some innovative idea of the Apostle. Rather, the picture of God as the husband of Israel is found throughout the Tanach. So if we want a picture of the highest ideal of what a husband should be, we may search out the various characteristics of God as He presents Himself as a husband. The fact that we may acutely sense our own lacks and inabilities, and therefore despair at ever reaching such a high ideal should not deter us from recognizing God Himself as the pattern we long to follow. Our goal is to follow in the footsteps of our Master, and to be conformed to His way of doing things. Therefore, the picture of God as husband stands ever before us as the goal we strive to attain.

In this regard, we must understand that there is a distinction between the marriage relationship and all other familial relationships. While all other familial relationships occur as a product of natural events, the marriage relationship is a direct gift of God to mankind. When Adam was naming the animals, and in so doing, looking for a companion, he was looking for something that existed innately within the created order. Of course, he found nothing in the animal kingdom to satisfy his need for a companion. When Chavah was fashioned by God, however, he did realize that she corresponded directly to him, and that therefore there was a possibility of genuine companionship. Yet the most important aspect of the relationship is signalled when God brings Chavah to Adam. The relationship that was to ensue was not something that was innate within the created order, but was a direct gift from the hand of the Almighty.

Let me illustrate this with the Sabbath. In the natural order of the created world, the heavenly bodies govern the passage of time. The sun marks the turn of the year and seasons, the boundaries of day and night, and the moon marks the span of a month. Were one to be marooned alone on some remote island, they could determine the span of a year, the span of a month, and the beginning and end of the day. These periods of time are innate within the creative order. But one could never tell exactly, at least just by looking at the sun and moon, which day was the Sabbath. This is because the Sabbath does not exist as the function of the created order, but as a direct gift of God to mankind. Only as one receives the Sabbath as a gift from God may they continue to mark the seven-day week, and reckon the Sabbath.

In the same way, marriage is a gift from God. The idea that one man and one woman would covenant together for life, to intertwine their lives and meld them into one, is not something taught in the created world—it is the gift of the Creator. The importance of this cannot be over estimated! Whenever we see, in the course of human history, a disregard for God and His revelation of truth, we also see the demise of the gift of marriage. In our own times, when the rule of God—indeed, even His very existence—is considered a myth of naive minds, the relationship of marriage is diminished, and even destroyed in favor of redefinitions that entirely undermine the very essence of marriage.

I say all of this to emphasize a very important fact: only when we accept God's perspective, and receive marriage from Him as a gift, will we be able both to appreciate what marriage is, and have great motivation to nurture and maintain it. As husbands, we must view our relationship of marriage as the gift of God to us—a supreme gift of immeasurable value. When viewed in this way, we will be far more willing to expend the necessary spiritual, emotional, and physical efforts required to make our marriage what God intends.

The Characteristics of God as Husband

1. Faithfulness

When we read of God's relationship to Israel, His chosen people, under the rubric of the marriage relationship, one of the primary characteristics we encounter is that of faithfulness.

Perhaps the most elaborate picture of this is found in the prophet Hosea. This entire prophecy is presented in dramatic fashion as a picture of Israel's unfaithfulness to God, acting out her waywardness as an unfaithful wife. Yet like the prophet himself, who is instructed to purchase his harlot wife, God remains faithful to Israel in spite of her religious adultery.

> Hos. 11:12 Ephraim surrounds Me with lies and the house of Israel with deceit; Judah is also unruly against God, even against the Holy One who is faithful.

Likewise, Jeremiah speaks of Israel's unfaithfulness, casting her debauchery in the metaphor of marriage. Her sin has caused a breach, even a divorce in her relationship to the Almighty. Yet God does not abandon her, nor go looking for someone to take her place. Instead, in His faithfulness to Israel, He calls her back:

> Jer 3:22 "Return, O faithless sons, I will heal your faithlessness." "Behold, we come to You; For You are the Lord our God.

Thus, the promise of God's faithfulness to Israel, in spite of her own unfaithfulness, is promised early in the book of Hosea:

> Hos. 2:19 "I will betroth you to Me forever; yes, I will betroth you to Me
> in righteousness and in justice, in lovingkindness and in compassion …

This over arching characteristic of faithfulness is at the heart of the marriage covenant, and thus is the foundation upon which the life of a Godly husband is built.

What are the components of the characteristic of faithfulness? In general, faithfulness means remaining true to one's vows and the responsibilities demanded by such vows. Faithfulness in marriage means faithfulness to the covenant of marriage (which is why the marriage metaphor is so well suited to paint the picture of God's relationship to Israel). This means, first of all, that a husband must be willing to lay down his life for his wife. By speaking of "laying down" one's life, I do not mean only the willingness to physically protect one's wife even to death. That, of course, would be the supreme indication of faithfulness. But besides the ultimate sacrifice of giving one's physical life to protect his wife, I mean the willingness to give up one's own personal comforts and desires for the needs of one's wife. This is what Paul means when he speaks of husbands loving their wives as Messiah loved His *kehilah,* "and gave Himself up for her." Granted, the death of the Messiah upon the execution stake was that ultimate "giving," but His having given Himself up for His bride entailed much more than that. His willingness to leave the glory of heaven, to take upon Himself the confinement of human flesh, to bear the sorrows and woes of this fallen world—all of this He willingly did in order to love His bride. He literally went from riches to rags in order to make His bride wealthy:

> 2Cor. 8:9 For you know the grace of our Lord Yeshua Messiah, that though
> He was rich, yet for your sake He became poor, so that you through His
> poverty might become rich.

If, then, we take the pattern of God as husband, and we focus on the attribute of faithfulness, we see that one component of faithfulness *is the willingness to die to self for the sake of the one loved.*

But while we may applaud the attribute of faithfulness as one of the necessary characteristics of a Godly husband, we must quickly note that faithfulness is not something we come by naturally. Faithfulness must be cultivated, nurtured, and established in one's life through diligent practice and resolve. How do we grow in faithfulness? How do we train ourselves to be faithful?

First, as men who either are husbands, or who are anticipating marriage in the future, we must practice the discipline of self-denial. Our Master said that if we should be His disciples, we must "deny ourselves, take up His cross daily, and follow Him" (Matt. 16:24; Mark 8:34; Luke 9:23). We may note some specific areas of our lives where such self-denial is so very important:

   a.   in relationship to *time*: am I willing to rearrange my own schedule in order to serve my wife?
   b.   in relationship to *money*: am I willing to put the needs of my wife and family ahead of my own desire for things; for my "hobby;" for my own pleasure and entertainment?
   c.   in relationship to *comfort*: am I willing to accept the responsibility of difficult situations, shielding my wife from the stress of problems, or do I let her deal with the uncomfortable things?

It is apparent that if a man has not learned the spiritual duty of self-denial, and if he does not grow in his ability to maintain a life of self-denial, he will be unable to live out the life of faithfulness that marks a Godly husband. Learning to deny one's self for the good of others comes in the small things, which, when practiced time and time again, give the ability to deny oneself in the larger things. Never despise the small ways in which you may put your wife first. These are "daily conditioning" that allows you to gain strength in the realm of faithfulness as a husband.

Secondly, a man who intends to display faithfulness as a Godly husband must discipline himself in his own spiritual growth. Faithfulness, as I said, is not something we come by naturally. It is a spiritual dimension. Thus, as husbands, we must nourish our own souls in our relationship to God through the Messiah Yeshua. This means:

   a.   hiding God's word in my heart: do I consider the nourishment of the word of God in my own life just as necessary as the physical nourishment I require?
   b.   spending time in prayer: do I regularly seek God's help for spiritual strength, guidance, and wisdom? Am I learning communion with God through times of prayer?

    c. praising God: am I willing to praise God openly? Am I giving Him the "sacrifice of praise?"

    d. Godly friendships: do I see and appreciate the value of Godly community as the means of being built up spiritually?

Thirdly, cultivating faithfulness as a husband entails a negative aspect as well: keeping oneself from the temptations of the world, particularly in the area of sexual lust. Positively, we must practice self-denial and spiritual disciplines. Negatively, we must guard ourselves from the draw of the world. Our society has almost no moral values remaining. Our entire world is encompassed with sexually explicit advertising, movies, music, and fashions. In our work-a-day world, a constant appeal is made to our flesh—drawing our passions to be aroused and spent on the fleeting pleasures of the world. We are fools if we think we are impervious to these attacks. Still remaining within us is the draw to that which we know is wrong. Therefore, we must constantly be aware of the battle in which we are engaged, and be prepared to withstand the fiery arrows of the enemy of our souls.

How do we do this? What are the spiritual disciplines in which we must engage in order to be victorious in this battle?

    a. we must know who we are in Messiah (Rom 6): the draw that we may feel to the things of this world is our flesh, not our genuine selves. We have been remade in the image of Messiah. If we are honest with ourselves, we know that in our hearts we long to please our Master. It is the flesh—the sinful nature that remains within—that we war against. So we must learn to be who we are, not who we use to be.

    b. we must guard ourselves from the schemes of the evil one (Eph 6:10ff): situations that put us into the place of temptation are the traps of this world. The wise man refuses to be put in such situations; the fool thinks he's "strong enough."

    c. we must know that our true strength is in God: admitting our weakness makes us strong. A humble heart receives strength; an arrogant heart is always vulnerable. "God resists the proud, but gives grace to the humble" (Prov 3:34; James 4:6; 1Pet 5:5).

Finally, faithfulness as a husband requires courage and boldness.

The media of our day generally portrays husbands as ignorant, self-serving, self-centered, and out of touch with the family. Unfortunately, this *persona* of husbands (and men in general) has been accepted as the norm. "That's just the way men are!" No! That's the way weak men are. Men of strength are men of character, who remain faithful under fire. It is not difficult to see such character in men during times of war. The willingness to remain faithful in the face of overwhelming odds was displayed by firefighters, law enforcement personnel, government officials, and the military in the recent attacks upon our nation. These men were raised up as national heros in the wake of 9/11. And rightly so. But what we often fail to realize is that a similar kind of battle is being fought over the family. Remaining faithful as a husband will require the same kind of stick-to-itivness as a soldier in battle. If we will be faithful husbands, we must commit ourselves to faithfulness without any excuses or "back doors." Our calling is to be men of resolve who will remain faithful regardless of the personal cost. It is in this commitment that true manliness is portrayed.

Paul notes in 1Cor 4:2 that "…it is required of stewards that one be found trustworthy (πιστός, *pistos*, 'faithful')." A steward is one to whom something of high value has been entrusted. As husbands, we have been entrusted with the care and life of our wives. We must therefore commit ourselves to this happy responsibility with true resolve and unflinching commitment. Moreover, such commitment is itself powerful, for when we commit ourselves to what God has commanded, we may trust that He will supply the necessary strength.

2. Caring

God, as the husband of Israel, is portrayed in the Tanach as One who displayed tender care for Israel:

Jer. 31:31 "Behold, days are coming," declares the Lord, "when I will make a new covenant with the house of Israel and with the house of Judah, 32 not like the covenant which I made with their fathers in the day I took them by the hand to bring them out of the land of Egypt, My covenant which they broke, although I was a husband to them," declares the Lord.

Zeph 3:17 "The Lord your God is in your midst, a victorious warrior. He will exult over you with joy, He will be quiet in His love, He will rejoice over you with shouts of joy.

Jeremiah pictures God as a husband to Israel, leading her by the hand out of the slavery of Egypt. In another metaphor, Zephaniah portrays God as a mighty warrior, coming home from the victory of the battle, reunited with His wife. He is "quiet in His love," rejoicing over His wife with "shouts of joy."

These metaphors of God as the ideal husband of Israel bear stark contrasts. In both cases, God is pictured as a warrior who defeats the enemy (Egypt, the nations), yet who is gentle and caring—a mighty warrior who knows how to be "quiet in His love."

A Godly husband has strength while at the same time is able to be gentle and caring. This same idea is found in Paul's admonition to husbands in Eph 5:25f:

> 25 Husbands, love your wives, just as Messiah also loved His *kehilah* and gave Himself up for her, 26 so that He might sanctify her, having cleansed her by the washing of water with the word, 27 that He might present to Himself the congregation in all her glory, having no spot or wrinkle or any such thing; but that she would be holy and blameless.

The giving of Himself for His bride is viewed as cleansing her by washing, and repairing and cleaning her soiled garments so that she may be publicly displayed in all of her beauty.

In each of these pictures, the wife has needs that the caring Husband sees, understands, and meets. In Jeremiah, Israel is enslaved, and God leads her out of her slavery, holding her hand. In Zephaniah, Israel is under siege by her enemies, and God comes as a warrior, defeating her foes, and embracing her in the protection of His victory. In Ephesians 5, Paul describes the wife as wearing tattered and soiled clothes. The Husband washes her, and clothes her with garments of perfection. Surely the meaning in each case is primarily that of spiritual cleansing—of bringing righteousness where there was sin. But the metaphors of marriage used in each case only "work" if, in fact, this is the basic approach of a husband toward his wife, i.e., that the husband carefully and gently meets the needs of his wife.

It is clear that there is a progression here. We began by noting the attribute of faithfulness. This requires self-denial on the part of the husband, a willingness to put his own needs as secondary to those of his wife. Such a perspective on the part of a husband puts him in the proper mindset to see his wife's needs, and therefore to meet them. Conversely, a husband who is self-absorbed will have little ability to focus upon the needs of his wife.

But a husband who commits himself to meeting the needs of his wife through gentle, consistent caring, cannot do so if he is unaware of her needs. Meeting the needs of one's wife, therefore, requires constant attention and communication. We all are aware of the downward cycle that begins when communication stops. When a husband and his wife withdraw from each other and stop communicating, the needs of the wife and husband go unattended by each other. This increases the animosity between them, and further isolation ensues. The only remedy is to restore communication, and the willingness to hear and be heard.

But who breaks the cycle of stopped communication? We may take our que, once again, from the manner in which God presents Himself as husband to Israel. Throughout the history of the nation, Israel's disobedience to God's commands brought about a breach in their covenant relationship. Israel turned away from listening to God and went her own way. But God's response is not to abandon her, nor to remain silent toward her. On the contrary: He sends His prophets time and again to call her back, promising her His willingness to forgive and bring about restoration.

As men who desire to be Godly husbands, we too must be willing to take the initiative in restoring communication. Sometimes this is the most difficult step, but it is also the most important. Allowing time to go by when there is an obvious need to talk and seek forgiveness, will only make restoration more difficult. Our strength of character will be seen in our willingness to humbly approach our wife and seek to rectify whatever wrong has taken place.

Being a caring husband means taking an active role in being aware of your wife's needs. That requires understanding that the needs of a woman are far different than those of a man. All too often men think that if they provide the physical needs of their wife and family, they are fulfilling the role of provider. Men may presume that their wife's definition of "needs" is the same as theirs. But that is clearly not the case.

Years ago I was approached by a young couple who were having difficulty in their marriage. They asked if they could spend some time talking with me about the problem they were encountering. When we met, the husband explained that he was working hard, bringing home a pay check, paying the bills, and generally providing for his wife. But he felt that she did not appreciate all of the hard work and sacrifice he was giving in order to provide for their needs. The wife explained that after coming home from a hard day's work, her husband ate dinner, watched some TV, and then went to bed. She felt like they were better friends before they were married than after. She explained that she felt unappreciated and more like a housemaid than a wife. After listening to each of them, I asked how often they sat in the evenings and just talked to each other about the events of the day. They admitted they hardly ever did that any more. So I "prescribed" this requirement: for the next two weeks, each evening after dinner, she was to sit on his lap and they were to spend at least 15 minutes talking about the events of the day. A month later they returned for a scheduled time of counseling, and I could tell a lot had changed! They were holding hands, and had smiles on their faces. He explained that he hadn't realized how much his wife was doing during the day, and how much time it took to keep the house so clean and neat the way he liked it. But the wife's statement was revealing: she said all she really wanted was to be hugged again, the way she was when they first were married. And they both admitted that 15 minutes was not nearly long enough, and that they were now spending a lot longer than that in their after-dinner ritual.

The point I want to make in this illustration (and I wish I could say marriage difficulties were always resolved this easily!) is that what the husband thought were his wife's needs, clearly were not. He viewed her needs primarily as physical, because that was how he defined his own needs. But her needs were more acutely emotional rather than physical. She had the need to be embraced and reassured of her husband's caring love. When he took the time to do that, he was able to share with his wife how hard his work was, and that, in turn, gave her a greater appreciation for the stress under which he labored. In the end, the distance they had built between each other was overcome by a commitment to expressing a genuine care for each other in the context of simply spending time together, and talking.

3. Leading

If we continue to look at the character of God as husband to Israel, and therefore as the supreme model for all husbands to follow, we see how God fulfilled the role of *Leader* in His marriage covenant with Israel. As noted above, Jeremiah 31:31-34, which uses the metaphor of God as

Israel's husband, pictures Him taking Israel "by the hand" and leading her out of Egypt. Taking a leadership role in the marriage relationship is clearly an important aspect of being a Godly husband.

Men obviously have different personalities and personal traits. Some are more extravert and others introvert. But regardless of one's personality makeup, every man can and should fulfill a leadership role within the marriage. Paul writes in 1Cor 11:3, "But I want you to understand that Messiah is the head of every man, and the man is the head of a woman, and God is the head of Messiah." This statement may seem puzzling at first, but in the context its overall import is clear: each looks to the "head" for direction—for leadership.

This does not negate the obvious fact that the wife also has leadership roles within the marriage, but it means that in the overall perspective of things, the husband is to take the responsibility of leadership. If one were to ask where the "buck stops" in a marriage, it is with the husband. Even though decision making surely involves both the husband and wife working together, the husband needs to provide a leading role in overall direction of the family.

If we bear in mind what we have learned from the Genesis account of the fall of mankind into sin, we will reckon with the fact that a woman, seeking a place of security, will naturally want to formulate a plan—even take the lead to make sure issues of the home and family are ordered and in place. Conversely, it seems as though often the natural tendency of a man is to look after himself and neglect to provide leadership for his wife and family. The less a man provides leadership within the marriage and family, the greater is the tendency for the wife to take up a leadership role in his place. This "flip-flopped" arrangement may seem to work at first. The woman is assured of things being in order, because she plans them to be so. Likewise, the husband is content to let his wife do the planning and leading since it lets him "off the hook." His fear of failure is diminished since his wife is taking the lead.

But in the long run, this arrangement does not work. This is because fundamentally, leadership involves authority. Usually, a husband who neglects the difficult task of leading, and apathetically allows his wife to take the responsibility of leading the family, still expects to remain the head (authority) of his home. He wants to have his cake and eat it too. What he finds out, however, is that when his wife is doing the hard work of leading, she also expects to have the authority that goes along with her role as leader.

On the other hand, a woman who accepts the leadership role in the family thinks that she will have the security of an orderly home (because she's in control), but in reality, she takes upon herself a role of authority that her husband should shoulder, a role that brings her undue stress and discontent.

Nowhere is this problem seen more than in the handling of finances within the marriage. Statistics tell us (if we can trust statistics) that the single greatest cause of divorce in the early years of a marriage is finances. Let's face it: for the majority of people, the money never seems sufficient for the needs. And therefore, deciding how money is to be spent becomes a constant battle. If a wife is in charge of the finances, she takes upon herself the role of "decider" in matters that affect the whole family, including her husband. Moreover, some of the greatest stress in a marriage comes when there is insufficient funds to meet all of the monthly bills. A wife who is in charge of the finances must also shoulder the stress that results from poor financial decisions, which usually result in debt and the inability to pay for that debt. When the creditors begin to call, asking when payment will be made, she is the one who must bear the constant burden of "how to make ends meet."

What adds to this problem is the fact that many times, women are better at administrative tasks than men. Women tend to be more organized and keeping track of bills, bank accounts, and budgets seems at times to be better handled by the wife than the husband.

But a husband who is willing to take upon himself the God-given role of leader within the marriage, will also take the responsibility of the finances, and find ways to accomplish the task in order to shield his wife from the stress that money matters inevitably bring.

I am not suggesting, however, that it is an "either-or" situation. When the husband takes the responsibilities of the finances, he does so as a partner with his wife. Financial decisions should be made together, since these decisions will affect the entire family. But what I mean by the husband taking the responsibilities of the finances is that he both disciplines himself to make good financial choices, and that he also bears the responsibility (and thus the stress) of the financial health of the family. We will talk more about the "how" of financial leadership in a subsequent lesson, but for now, I simply want to stress that part of the leadership role of a Godly husband involves his owning the financial responsibilities of the family.

In our modern world, this issue of finances became far more significant as the feminist movement gained momentum. As more and more women left the home to work and to seek careers, they likewise were "empowered" financially. It became the norm for a wife and husband to have separate bank accounts, and to make financial decisions independent of each other. Since the husband and wife were now working for "their own money," the sticky issue of who pays for what becomes a new cause of division between them. And while this scenario is not always the case, in the majority of households where both the husband and wife work outside of the home, their lives became more and more individualistic as each seeks to reach his or her own financial goals.

Surely there are exceptions, but the norm as found in the Scriptures is that the husband works to provide for the needs of the family, and the wife fulfills her role as the primary nurturer of the children, transforming a dwelling place (house) into a home where God's shalom could be experienced by the whole family.

This norm is clearly presupposed in Paul's admonition to the older women (Titus 2:3–5):

> Older women likewise are to be reverent in their behavior, not malicious gossips nor enslaved to much wine, teaching what is good, so that they may encourage the young women to love their husbands, to love their children, *to be* sensible, pure, workers at home, kind, being subject to their own husbands, so that the word of God will not be dishonored.

This is not merely a sociological, cultural issue, as though Paul is referring to something that obtained only in the ancient Israelite culture of the 1st Century. If we contextualize this admonition to pertain only to his time and not ours, we undermine the eternal relevance of the Scriptures. Rather, the Apostle's teaching is based upon what he conceived of as the normal family: the husband works to provide the needs of the family, and the wife fulfills the high calling of loving her husband, her children, and creating a home where the word of God is honored.

The role of a Godly husband in being a leader obviously extends far beyond the handling of finances. He must also take the lead in spiritual matters. Once again, this does not at all negate the leadership role of the wife in spiritual matters. Indeed, the Godly wife plays a strategic and crucial role in teaching the way of God to her family. But the role of the husband as a spiritual leader involves making sure that the ways of God are firmly in place, and that all things necessary for growing in faith and love for God are provided. As noted before, this means that a Godly husband is maturing in his own faith. He cannot expect to lead and present a model of faith to his family if he is not maintaining a fervent, growing relationship with his Master.

This spiritual leadership incumbent upon the husband is taught in the Torah. In Numbers 30:3ff, the vow of a wife or daughter can be overturned by her father or husband if done so immediately. This makes it clear that the father/husband has a leadership role in terms of spiritual matters such as vows. But it also highlights the point that the father or husband must be "in tune" with what is going on in his family. He acts as a protector for wife and daughter, in that his ability to annul a rash vow is honored by the Lord (Num 30:8). Note that in this same Torah text, the vow of a widow or divorced woman stands (30:9), for in her situation, she has no spiritual authority over her for a covering.

4. Communicating

When we consider the relationship of God and Israel under the metaphor of a marriage, we are struck with the fact that He is seen as a communicator. Humbling Himself to the confines of human language, He wrote His own letter of instruction (the Torah) to Israel. Moreover, He sent His prophets with His words of instruction, promise, and warning. In the most majestic of ways, He communicated His heart to His bride.

Men are often characterized as non-communicative. This, of course, is not the case for all men, but it seems to be true of most. Men simply have more difficulty communicating their thoughts than women do, most specifically because communicating one's inner feelings and thoughts makes one vulnerable. In general, men tend to be more private. In contrast, women have a greater need to talk about what they feel and think. These general tendencies are a sure recipe for problems if they are not realized and overcome.

What often happens is this: a wife needs times of heart-to-heart communication with her husband, something he tends to resist. As he resists, the wife tries to find ways to affect such communication. She withdraws, hoping he'll ask what's bothering her, or she nags, hoping he'll give into talking with her, or she yells, thinking that he'll respond in self-defense. Most often, however, these tactics just push her husband away. Her attempts at opening lines of communication seem futile and even counter-productive. If she finally decides her efforts are worthless, the non-communication continues and the relationship falls on hard times.

A Godly husband, however, should realize from the beginning that constant communication with his wife is an essential aspect of meeting her needs. He must find regular times to express what is actually going on in his life: his plans, hopes, dreams, weaknesses, and fears. And he must be honestly concerned about his wife's thoughts, dreams, hopes, and fears. So he must take the lead in communication, not waiting for his wife always to initiate the conversation.

Men may consider such disclosure as a sign of weakness, but it is not. Genuine communication to one's wife is a matter of a love, honesty, and humility. If we are committed to loving our wives as Messiah loves His bride (Eph 5:25f), then we must greatly desire to know what she is thinking and feeling. This requires communication. Moreover, communicating the deeper issues of life as we are experiencing them assures our wives that they are an integral part of our lives, and that we trust them and rely upon them as our closest friend. Note well that in the description of the "Woman of Valor" (Prov 31:10ff), the response of the husband is described this way (v. 11): "The heart of her husband trusts in her, and he will have no lack of gain." What exactly does this "trust" entail? It means that one is not afraid to let one's wife into his heart. Finding ways to communicate one's true self through regular and careful means will strengthen the relationship of marriage by building the deep friendship it is intended to be.

Summary

In this very brief overview, we have looked at the character of God as husband to Israel, and taken this metaphor as suggesting the norm for a Godly husband. We have summed up these characteristics under four main headings: faithfulness, caring, leading, and communicating. We can summarize general characteristics as follows:

Faithfulness:
1. remaining true to my vows no matter what it costs
2. sacrificing my own wants for the sake of meeting the needs of my

wife
3. learning to deny myself
4. maturing in my faith and gaining spiritual strength
5. keeping myself from the snares of the world
6. growing in courage and boldness to face the battles of life

Caring:

1. paying close attention to the needs of my wife
2. expressing gentleness as a part of manly strength
3. taking the initiative to restore broken communication
4. building a deepening friendship by giving my wife priority

Leading:

1. taking the responsibilities of leadership in order to protect and nurture my wife
2. bearing the responsibilities of finances
3. taking the role of provider for my wife and family
4. putting the spiritual health of my wife and family as a top priority

Communicating:

1. initiating regular times of verbal communication with my wife
2. opening my own life to my wife, including my weaknesses and fears
3. trusting that my wife has been given to me by God in order to make me the man He wants me to be

Let's Talk About It!

1. What factors in our society, do you think, contribute most to the breakdown of Godly character in men?

2. Why is a man often hesitant to communicate openly with his wife?

3. What are the consequences of breaking one's vows? (cf. Deut

23:21; Mal 1:14; Ps 15:4; 50:14; Matt 5:33–37)

4. Consider the teaching of our Master in Luke 16:10 "He who is faithful in a very little thing is faithful also in much; and he who is unrighteous in a very little thing is unrighteous also in much." Discuss how this principle works in terms of young men preparing for marriage.

5. As a daughter and her parents look for a man suitable to be her husband, what things indicate the man's ability to be faithful?

6. What kinds of things do women generally consider very important, which men may consider unimportant?

7. What kinds of things do men generally consider very important which women may consider unimportant?

8. Discuss the difference between "needs" and "wants." How can a husband discern between the actual "needs" of his wife, as opposed to things that his wife "wants?" When do "wants" become "needs?"

Chapter 6
Characteristics of a Godly Wife

When we ask ourselves how the Torah describes a godly wife, we begin, as we did when considering the character of a godly husband, with the foundational statement of Moses in Genesis 2:24: "For this reason a man shall leave his father and his mother, and be joined to his wife; and they shall become one flesh." As noted above (pp. 20ff), the marriage covenant between a man and his wife is characterized by the man *leaving* father and mother, *being joined* to his wife, resulting in the two *becoming one*. Note that the initial action (leaving) is done by the man, not the woman. But the subsequent verb ("joining," דבק, *dabaq*) necessarily involves both the man and woman, and the result is likewise mutual: "they shall become one flesh." The wife therefore takes an active role in the process of being joined together with her husband, resulting in their oneness.

But it is obvious in the creation narrative that God is the One who prepares Chavah for Adam. While Adam obviously had a natural sense of what would be required for companionship (he didn't find what he needed in any of the animals he named), God was the One who knew best what was needed to overcome Adam's deficiency defined as "being alone," a situation labeled as "not good" (Gen 2:18). To put it simply, when God fashioned Chavah, He did so in order to make mankind what they were intended to be. Adam by himself could never represent God as the image bearer He intended. In order for mankind to accomplish their creative purpose, male and female, joined together as one, was absolutely necessary.

The godly wife must therefore begin with this important perspective: her role is essential, not merely complimentary. Her husband will never be able to accomplish his God-given purpose in life apart from her, nor will she be able to fulfill her life's purpose without him. It is in their unique ability to be one that they will find the joy of contentment in fulfilling their very purpose for existing.

I titled the previous chapter "Characteristics of a Godly Husband," and followed suit with this chapter heading, "Characteristics of a Godly Wife." The key term in both of these titles is "Godly." As we saw earlier, the entrance of sin into this world turned everything on its head. Adam became self-serving, offering excuses that impugned the goodness of God ("this woman You gave to me...," Gen 3:12) and Chavah sought to control the situation independently ("...she took from its fruit and ate...," Gen 3:6). Following the fall into sin, Adam thought being alone was a viable option, and Chavah thought being in charge was acceptable. Both were wrong. It is only when God's perspective is once again acknowledged and accepted that a return to the way things ought to be can be achieved. Thus, at the heart of biblical marriage is the spiritual dynamic of accepting God's way. That's what I mean by "Godly." This, of course, is a spiritual matter. The fallen nature does not want to accept God's revelation, nor does it want to conform to God's ways. A change of heart—a regeneration of the will—is therefore at the core of returning to marriage as God intended.

We all are affected by the society in which we live, and especially by the subtle but sometimes overwhelming philosophy or worldview that pervades a society. Like it or not, the *zeitgeist* (spirit of the times) is like a toxic substance that enters our thought process through a kind of philosophical osmosis. The only hope for us is that we may take captive every thought and filter it through the eternal, unchanging truth of God's revelation.

This is particularly true with regard to the feminist movement so prevalent in our times. This is not to suggest that the so-called feminist movement is entirely without merit, or that the reasons for its growth are not real. It is clearly the case that when human society gives way to the base impulses of men, women are marginalized and misused. Or to put it another way, when the ethics of the Scriptures are rejected, women and children are the first and most evident to be affected. In some ways, then, the current feminist movement is a reaction against abuse and marginalization by a male dominance within our own wayward society.

But the current feminist movement is a reaction against such abuse from a mostly humanistic standpoint. It is an ungodly response to a very real problem. The feminist movement is an attempt to raise the value of women by diminishing the value of men. The only lasting solution to the problem of misogyny is a return to God's truth about the relationship of male and female, something that can happen only when we submit to God in faith, and trust that His ways are right.

How has the feminist movement in our times affected the way we think? First, the feminist movement strives for equality between men and women on the bases of personal independence. The value of a woman is seen as her ability to exist independent of a man, standing in her own value apart from anyone else. To this notion we could apply the same assessment given by the Almighty in the case of Adam: "it is not good for woman to be alone." Putting the emphasis upon the independent value of a woman, the feminist movement has fallen into the same trap of the enemy that snared Adam and Chavah. God did not create us to be independent. He created us for each other.

Secondly, the feminist movement puts the emphasis upon personal achievement and is disgusted with the idea of serving others from a humble heart. The very idea that a woman should humbly serve a man is considered to be the core problem. Yet our own Master taught us that the one who serves is the greatest of all (Matt 20:26). Being a servant is not a menial position in God's eyes, but one of great value and worth. This, of course, is just as true for men as for women. The characteristics of a godly husband are all grounded upon his willingness to be a servant to his wife. But it is equally true for the godly wife: she must realize that serving her husband is the path to true oneness.

Thirdly, and following close on the heels of this idea of humble service, the feminist movement in our times has degraded the value of domestic tasks for women. Trying to achieve equality with males by seeking similar roles with them, women have left the home, despised motherhood, and sought careers promising power and financial independence. The effect of this shift in our society has not, however, resulted in women experiencing greater fulfillment and peace of mind. The increased stress upon women, the breakdown of the family, and the neglect of children have so fractured our society that one wonders if we have moved beyond the point of return. What were accepted norms even 25 year ago have all but been forgotten, and as a result our worldview has been reshaped and reinterpreted from presuppositions that are blatantly ungodly. Women who desire to fulfill their God-given role as set forth in the Scriptures must regain the high value put upon home and children. Consider how high and strategic is the divine call upon mothers, who are able to mold and shape the very souls of their children, and create a home where the shalom of God provides the necessary solace in which a family can blossom and bear godly fruit. It is no exaggeration to say that true Torah community has as a cornerstone that work of wives and mothers in fashioning and preserving the family, the very building blocks of community and society itself. No career, regardless of its prestige within the society, can equal the value of a diligent wife and mother who, with much wisdom and hard work, turns a house into a home.

Finally, the feminist movement in our time has sought to degrade men. As a result, it is not uncommon in our times to see an emphasis against marriage and for singleness. Again, I do not mean to suggest that singleness is wrong. In fact, according to Paul (1Cor 7:26ff), singleness may even be encouraged in some instances. Yet we know that God instituted marriage, and that He has given it as the norm. The feminist movement, on the other hand, has sought to cast men in such negative ways as to bring into question whether marriage is even desirable. For many feminists, men are a liability. Add to this that children are more and more "raised" in day care because Mom is off pursuing her career, and we are left with no desirable model of "family" worth pursuing. Many children in our society have no idea what a godly marriage and home looks like. Why marry and have children if that only stands in the way of one's own career choices, or if marriage and children only result in unending strife?

Women who desire to be godly wives and mothers must therefore seek diligently to retool their perspectives away from the prevailing societal *zeitgeist* and bring them in line with the divine revelation of God's word. Regardless of how "provincial" or "outmoded" the role of women in the Scriptures may appear when set against the backdrop of the modern worldview, women of faith, strength, and courage must give themselves to the ways of the Almighty. In so doing, they will surely discover the joy and fulfillment that accompanies humble obedience.

Role Models

In Peter's first epistle, he suggests that the matriarchs provide a fitting role model for a woman who seeks to fulfill her God-given role as a wife (cf. 1Pet 3:5–6). This does not mean that all of the actions of the matriarchs are worthy, nor that in every way they provide a role model to follow. But it does suggest that we would do well to consider the example of the matriarchs, and glean from them some characteristics of godly wives.

Interestingly, Yitzchak is one of the only patriarchs who, according to the Genesis narrative, had only one wife. It seems fitting, then, that we should look at their marriage, and specifically at Rivka's role as a wife, to discern patterns to be followed.

In Genesis 24, we are given the story of Avraham's servant, (was it Eliezer?), as he is commissioned to go and find a wife for Yitzchak. His work is done with a full reliance upon God to lead him to the right woman (24:12). The story is well known: Rivka comes to water the livestock, and, in accordance with the servant's prayer, she offers not only to give him water, but also to water his camels. By this he knows that she is the chosen one. Rivka takes him to the house of her father Bethuel, where he relates the whole story, and seeks the hand of Rivka to be the wife of his master, Yitzchak. Because of the supernatural manner in which the events occurred, it is clear to all that God has made the choice: Rivka is to be Yitzchak's wife. After exchanging gifts and essentially finalizing the transaction with Bethuel, Rivka herself is consulted. Her response to the question "Will you go with this man?" is short and clear: "I will go."

This whole story seems entirely foreign to us. How is it possible that a father sends a servant to find a wife for his son, and that the entire matter seems to be done without the direct input of either the future husband or wife? Obviously, the narrative is compacted, and we are not privy to all of the conversations. Yet one thing stands out as prominent: both Yitzchak and Rivka demonstrate a great trust in their parents and in God's ability to direct the situation. Rivka watches as her future is decided, yet she apparently recognized the clear leading of the Lord in the whole matter. She does not hesitate to act upon that which she understands is God's will, even though it means leaving the protection of her home and family, and going with a total stranger to marry someone she's never met! If we see nothing else in this story, we should recognize her strong faith in God and in His ability to lead her in the right path.

The servant along with his men and Rivka arrive at the home of Avraham, and Yitzchak is walking in the field meditating (שׂוּחַ, *suach*). One has to imagine that what was foremost in his mind was the mission on which Avraham's servant had been sent. He had to be anxious about the young lady chosen to be his bride. When Rivka sees Yitzchak, she inquires of the servant who the man is, and she is informed that it is Yitzchak. Upon hearing this, she dismounts from her camel. Again, the narrative is compacted, but we can imagine her reason for doing this was to make herself ready to meet her future husband. The text explicitly states that she covered herself with her veil. In the Ancient Near East, there is no indication that women regularly wore veils, but it was not uncommon for a bride to be so adorned. The veil was a sign of purity, a sign that as a bride she was for the groom and no one else. Moreover, in this case, it was a sign of respect for Yitzchak. She was the chosen one for him, and she presented herself to him as one who had been kept for him and for him alone. The modern tradition of a bride wearing a veil may well find its origins here.

After the story of how the servant was lead to Rivka was related to Yitzchak, Rivka is taken to Sarah's tent, that is, to be welcomed by the other women of the clan. There she remained until the time of her actual marriage to Yitzchak. The story ends with the notice that Yitzchak married her and was comforted after the death of his mother, Sarah.

What characteristics of Rivka stand out in our story? First, she was a woman of strong character who was able to accept the leading of God, and make her decisions accordingly. Her simple statement "I will go" marks her as a woman with a strong yet humble character. She was not afraid to make a decision in accordance with what she saw as righteous and wise, and to follow through on that decision.

Secondly, she demonstrated her love for Yitzchak as the one chosen to be her husband by presenting herself as beautiful to him. If we are not reading too much between the lines, her dismounting was no doubt in order to prepare herself for meeting him the first time. We know from the subsequent narrative that she was beautiful (26:7), and we can surmise that she directed her beauty toward her chosen groom as she prepared to meet him. This arranged marriage had not diminished, in her eyes, the value of being attractive. The deep, personal, and romantic relationship that would be fostered between the two of them was still very much in place in spite of the legal arrangements that had been made.

Thirdly, she demonstrated her respect for Yitzchak. By veiling herself, she showed two things: that she was ready to be his bride, and that she had kept herself for him. This was no marriage of accommodation, nor simply something to which she had resigned herself. Though she had never met her husband-to-be, she already had committed herself to him, offering him the respect that comes from a heart of love.

These three characteristics: spiritual strength, beauty, and respect, are worthy of further elucidation.

Spiritual Strength

The characteristics of a godly wife are built upon a personal, growing relationship with God through faith in the Messiah, Yeshua. I think we all recognize that. It is important, however, for women to realize that their spiritual growth is a personal requirement. The idea that the study of the Scriptures, theological dialog and investigation, and spiritual development is the domain of men is clearly wrong. If a woman fails to grow in knowledge and grace of the Lord, she has no one to blame but herself. She must therefore discipline herself to the regular study of God's word, developing the skills necessary to understand and apply the Scriptures to her life and the lives of those she leads, including her husband. She must grow in godly wisdom, since she will often be called upon to apply such wisdom in the various roles she plays. This means she must engage herself in the spiritual disciplines of life, not allowing the many demands upon her time and energies to rob her of time with the Lord in prayer, worship, and study. It is from the strength of her own faith that she will be able to fulfill her duties as wife and mother.

Beauty

Some might question whether women need to be encouraged in the discipline of outward beauty. Some women are admittedly self-absorbed in regard to their appearance. Yet it is not uncommon that some women, after being married, fail to see the high value that outward beauty affords. Burdened with the necessary daily tasks of homemaking may leave a woman feeling like she really doesn't have time or energy to make herself attractive. Yet if she succumbs to such a mindset, she will have neglected a creative gift given to her by her Creator.

It is interesting to note how much is mentioned in the *'Eshet Chayil* (Prov 31:10ff) about adornment: v. 17 She girds herself with strength; v. 22 She makes coverings for herself, her clothing is fine linen and purple; v. 25 Strength and dignity are her clothing. This language of adornment shows that her outward appearance, which is beautiful, goes hand-in-hand with the inner beauty and strength that she possesses.

Paul gives an interesting apostolic command in 1 Tim 2:9, "Likewise, I want women to adorn themselves with proper clothing ...." The Greek is interesting, because the word translated "proper" (κοσμίω, *kosmio*) could just as well mean "that which evokes admiration or delight." In the context, the emphasis is put upon modesty and propriety, but it seems as though Paul is suggesting that women should dress with beauty in mind, always keeping to the guidelines of modesty. Thus, he is not suggesting that modest dress is dowdy and forlorn. On the contrary, Paul admonishes the women to dress with beautiful clothes that are modest, and thus portray the inner beauty of womanhood as God intends it.

In another place Paul writes that a woman's hair is her glory (1Cor 11:15). Apparently Paul expected that the style of a woman's hair should portray her femininity. This, of course, is somewhat cultural. Hair styles may differ from culture to culture, and from one generation to another. Regardless, in any given culture, the manner in which a woman wears her hair should be clearly feminine, and it should portray the glory of her womanhood. This means that there is a spiritual dimension regarding how a woman takes care of her hair.

After being married for a number of years, and having a number of children, a wife may presume that how she appears really makes little difference to her husband. After all, their marriage is well on its way, and the day is just too packed to afford any time for her personal makeup and adornments. So when her husband comes home from work and she greets him in her sweat pants and oversized, wrinkled t-shirt, that should be okay, at least she thinks so. And maybe it is, at least some of the time. But never forget that your husband loves to see you adorned as the beautiful person you truly are. Part of why he was attracted to you in the first place was because you let him see the beauty—you prepared yourself for him. Every woman can be beautiful to her husband. She just needs to see the value in that, and take the time it requires.

One more thing on this aspect of beauty and the godly wife. It is universally agreed upon that men are attracted by what they see. It's just the way men are made. In the work-a-day world, a man is regularly around women who are dressed for the workplace—most of them don't show up in baggy sweat pants and oversized t-shirts. They have learned that dressing up is to their advantage. So all day a godly man will discipline himself, guarding his eyes and keeping his heart. When he comes home and sees the beauty of his wife, he is strengthened all the more in his resolve to have a singleness of heart. Her beauty has helped him win the battle of thoughts.

Respect

Paul admonishes wives to "respect" their husbands (Eph 5:33). Actually the Greek word translated "respect" is φοβέω, *phobeo*, "to fear." In this case, the concept of "fear" means "show proper respect." What is the "proper respect" that a wife should have toward her husband? Is it really any different than the respect we should always show for one another? Not really. But the difference is in terms of degree and preference. A wife's respect for her husband should constantly tell him that he is number one in her heart and life. And whether a woman wants to believe it or not, that is something that is very important to her husband.

Something that is very powerful in the life of a man is when he knows that his wife is for him, supporting him in his endeavors, and anticipating his success. If, as I have suggested earlier, one of the fears that a man faces is the possibility of failure in what he is attempting to achieve, then a wife who is respecting his efforts is a great encouragement, and offers additional incentive for completing the tasks he has taken on. This means that a godly wife will not only be interested in her husband's work, but will also let him know how much she appreciates what he does, and that she is confident in his abilities to do his work well.

It is amazing how differently men and women approach life. What one considers very important, the other may think is trivial. Women will do well to understand that a man longs to be respected.

An event in my own life may illustrate this. When my wife and I were still courting, I would spend time at her home. We were both in college at the time, and her father was one of my professors. They lived not far from the campus, and so it was easy to leave my dorm room to spend the evening there. One evening I was at Paulette's house, doing some repairs on my car. The family was inside, and I was out in the cold garage, working on rebuilding the engine from my VW Bug. Suddenly Paulette came into the garage, sat on a stool beside the car, and asked how it was going. I asked her if she really wanted to be out in the cold garage, and she replied that she just wanted to see what I was doing, and how things were going. She remarked that she'd never seen an engine all torn apart, and that she was amazed that I could take it all apart and get it back together again! There she sat, interested in a bunch of nuts and bolts and engine parts. I couldn't believe it. Of course I realized that she wasn't that interested in VW mechanics—she was interested in me, and she wanted to be part of my life, even if it meant sitting in a cold garage with tools and engine parts scattered around. What is more, she was interested in a project I had undertaken, and she was convinced I could complete the task.

I don't suppose that event would be seen by most as a highlight in our courting days, but it was huge in my way of seeing things. Here was a wonderful woman who respected my feeble efforts to do a job that, admittedly, was something I wasn't sure I could do. But her confidence in me, and her desire to share life even at that level, was an indication of how committed she was to our relationship. Oh, and by the way, we drove that VW for the first years of our marriage!

I tell this little story just to illustrate how important it is for a wife to respect her husband. Understanding the challenges he faces in life, supporting him in those challenges, and encouraging him by expressing your confidence in him, will yield wonderful results in relationship building.

A Woman of Valor – Proverbs 31:10–31

When it comes to a catalog of virtues for a woman of high regard, none is more to the point than the praise given to the virtuous woman in Proverbs 31. It will be good for us, then, to briefly overview this poetic text as we seek the characteristics of a Godly wife.

The final chapters of Proverbs are said to be written by Agur the son of Jakeh (chapter 30) and King Lemuel (chapter 31). It is not certain who these individuals are, and much debate among the Sages and scholars has ensued over the issue. Rashi (along with other Jewish Sages), considered "Lemuel" (לְמוּאֵל) to be a cryptic or poetic form of "the mouth of God" (cf. Job 40:4, "Behold, I am insignificant; what can I reply to You? I lay my hand on my mouth" [יָדִי שַׂמְתִּי לְמוֹ־פִי]), and considered these words to be the words given to Solomon by his mother, revealed to her by God. (The Lxx has 31:10-31 following 29:27 without the notice regarding Lemuel). Most contemporary commentators take both Agur and Lemuel to be foreign masters of wisdom whose wise sayings were incorporated by the Israelite prophets, and were thus appended to the book of Proverbs. Regardless of the author, these words have found their way into the inspired Scriptures under the superintending hand of the Holy Spirit, and we may therefore trust them to teach us God's perspective regarding a virtuous woman.

The text we are studying (31:10-31) is an acrostic, each verse beginning with a successive letter of the Hebrew *aleph-bet*. Thus, it comes to us as a kind of "complete description," describing the virtuous woman "from A to Z." This "alphabetic" arrangement may also have facilitated memorization, particularly for young ladies who were being mentored as future wives.

10　　*An excellent wife, who can find? For her worth is far above jewels.* How should we understand the word חַיִל, *chayil*, translated here as "excellent," and in other English versions (e.g., NIV), as "noble character?" The word itself usually means "strength" or "power," and can also mean "wealthy," or someone having much property. The word often refers to an "army" or a "warrior" in battle. Most likely, the strong word is used here to describe a woman who possesses the many virtues necessary to perform her tasks as a wife and mother. Like the warrior who trains for battle and who possesses particular skills necessary for the battle, so the woman of valor has deep personal character, shown in her diligent life and disciplined ways that allow her to succeed in her most important position.

But such a woman is difficult to find—her value is more than one can imagine. This tells us that the virtues extolled here are those which are acquired, and that not every woman has set herself to achieve these characteristics. Moreover, coming at the end of a book like Proverbs, the list of virtues spoken of here are presented as the capstone of living according to wisdom.

11　　*The heart of her husband trusts in her, And he will have no lack of gain.* The Hebrew actually puts the word "trust" first in the sentence, and thus it acquires emphasis. The virtues of the Godly wife bring her husband to rely upon her. But it does not simply say that "her husband trusts in her," but "*the heart* of her husband trusts in her." This relationship of trust is far deeper than merely "working together." The husband willingly entrusts into her care matters of life which are most dear to him. He realizes that those things that are most precious are safe in her care. Rather than fearing that his wife will squander his estate, he has come to realize that by her diligence, his wife is the very source by which he is enriched. In the same way that the sheep relies upon the Shepherd, and thus lacks nothing (לֹא אֶחְסָר, Ps 23:1), so the husband of a virtuous wife has "no lack (חָסַר) of gain." The word translated "gain" (שָׁלָל) is usually found in the sense of "spoils of war," but here, used metaphorically, means that in the course of life, the Godly wife affords to her husband a boundless store of life's most important commodities.

12   *She does him good and not evil All the days of her life.* Here we have the general perspective of the virtuous woman: she has the good of her husband as the primary focus of the marriage, and she has committed herself to a life-long relationship of good. The word translated "does" is not the common term for "doing" (we would expect something like עָשָׂה or פָּעַל). Rather, it is the word גָּמַל, *gamal*, which is poetically appropriate here, for this word means "to bring," or better, "to bring to a completion," and is even used of "weaning" a child (cf. 1 Sam 1:23). It can also have the sense of "reward," as something given at the completion of a task. The NIV translates, "She brings him good, not harm, all the days of her life." Because of her inner strength, she succeeds in bringing her husband good and not harm as she goes about her daily tasks. The strength of her own heart is a ready solace for her husband.

Moreover, her strength is not here one day, and gone tomorrow. She is not captivated by trends and passing fancies. She knows who she is, and she acts in accordance with her character. She has the long-term in mind, and her actions bespeak this settled, unwavering resolve to accomplish her God-given role.

13   *She looks for wool and flax And works with her hands in delight.* The next verses pertain directly to her domestic role as homemaker and manager of the family. She takes seriously the high duty of clothing her family, and works skillfully to provide their temporal needs. Perhaps most important in this verse is the last word in the sentence (second to last in the Hebrew): "and works with her hands in *delight* (חֵפֶץ)." Her work is not a constant drudgery, even if at times it is not always pleasant. She delights in the work she is doing, not only because she has found a personal satisfaction in it, but because she realizes how essential it is for the well-being of her husband and family. Her many hours of learning the well-honed skills of homemaking have made her skillful at what she does, and she therefore finds real satisfaction in her work.

14   *She is like merchant ships; She brings her food from afar.* The woman of valor is not content with moderation—she seeks for the best. She is willing to go the extra mile (literally!) to find the necessary food that will grace the family table. To put it in modern terms, she is not satisfied with TV dinners, or (so-called) "fast food." Like the issue of clothing her family, she also takes great pride in nourishing them with food that is good for them, even though it requires additional work on her part (as the next verse indicates).

And if we can be allowed to take the metaphor a bit further, she, like a merchant, is both careful and shrewd (in the best sense of that word) in acquiring the produce she buys. She takes the time to find the best, and at the best possible price. That probably means that she's a skilled negotiator as well (especially when this notice is put back into the ancient world and the open markets in which food was sold).

15   *She rises also while it is still night and gives food to her household and portions to her maidens.* Here we see her dedication—even her own comforts are subservient to the needs of the household. One can imagine some in the family coming in late after working in the fields, or arriving home after a day of traveling. She interrupts her own sleep to make sure they are cared for. What is more, while she apparently has maidservants, she does not relegate these duties to them, but even serves them as well!

16   *She considers a field and buys it; From her earnings she plants a vineyard.* This verse has been used by some as a basis for the woman of the house engaging in business, in this case, buying real estate. But the Hebrew indicates something different. The word "considers" (זָמְם) means "to ponder" or "to plan," and the word translated "buys" is actually the common word "to take" (לָקַח). What this indicates is not that she has her eye open for real estate acquisition, but that most likely she considers a part of the land the family already owns, which is currently unproductive, and reclaims it for productive, arable land. We could imagine a rocky slope, or a parcel that is overgrown with weeds. She contemplates how it could be better used, and "takes" it or "reclaims" it. And then, from her own earnings (cf. v. 24), she buys the seedlings and plants a vineyard where before there was only useless property.

If we are to consider what this tells us of her character, it would speak to her creativity. The virtuous woman is not one who complains about not having enough room, or enough space to do what she needs to do. On the contrary, with wisdom and creativity, she takes what others consider as useless and transforms it into something productive for the whole family. In our modern world where most of us are city dwellers, this could be demonstrated by the creative use of space in our homes, or reclaiming what others would discard.

17   *She girds herself with strength And makes her arms strong.* Here we have more language that poetically fits with the idea of strength found in the opening word חַיִל, a "women of *valor.*" For the idea of "girding one's loins" (as the Hebrew has it) is the language of war, in which a warrior puts on his armor, or straps on his sword. Thus, the woman of virtue is seen here as one who is prepared for the hard work that her role demands. She is not overcome by the myriad of daily tasks and responsibilities she faces. Like a warrior prepared for battle, the strength of her character, and her resolve to excel at her duties, has equipped her to meet the challenges, difficult though they may be.

18   *She senses that her gain is good; Her lamp does not go out at night.* Literally, the Hebrew says, "She tastes (טָעַם) that her profits are good." That is, she rejoices in the success of her endeavors. She takes true delight in seeing that her work achieves its intended goal. Like a merchant who counts the daily till, and is gladdened by the profit he makes, so the virtuous woman is heartened to see the great benefit that comes as a result of her labors. Such a perspective only gives her new strength to continue on.

          If we were to put this in the realm of business, the virtuous woman acts like an entrepreneur rather than an employee. She has given herself to the success of the home to such an extent that she isn't "watching the clock" to see when she can finish. Her goal is to see the success of her labors, not simply to "put in her time."

19   *She stretches out her hands to the distaff, And her hands grasp the spindle.* We are obviously dealing with poetry here, so there are chiastic arrangements that require parallel thoughts. This verse parallels v. 13, in which she gathers wool and flax. Here, she engages in the actual tasks of spinning the wool in preparation of weaving it into cloth.

          But the wording also anticipates the next verse, as we are directed to the actions of her hands. Here, (as the Hebrew indicates), she "sends" (שָׁלַח) her hands to the distaff, and her hands grasp (טָמַד) the spindle." The idea of "sending" her hands envisions the quick and deliberate work of a skilled craftsman. The word "grasp" also has the sense of "support." The parallels to the next verse will be obvious, because her skill in providing for her own family extends beyond the confines of the home to others who are in need.

20   *She extends her hand to the poor, And she stretches out her hands to the needy.* Here, she "extends" (פָּרַשׂ) her hands, parallel to the former "grasp," giving the sense of "support" and "help." She likewise "stretches out" her hands (שִׁלַּח) or "sends" them to the poor.

Here we see the virtuous woman is ready to help those in need, in spite of the fact that her day is essentially consumed with the needs of her own family. For the woman of valor, there is always room for one more at the table, and those in need find in her a helping hand.

21   *She is not afraid of the snow for her household, For all her household are clothed with scarlet.* Even as the Proverbs tell us that the wise prepare for the future, and uses the ant as an example of preparing for the winter (6:6f), so the virtuous woman has made preparations for the winter, clothing her household in scarlet (שָׁנִים). Scarlet or crimson is not necessarily warmer than other clothing, so we wonder why it is used in this way. What appears to be the answer is this: the colorful garments, made with scarlet or crimson dyed thread, were outer garments, worn over the normal or common garments of the day. Thus, we should most likely understand this to mean that "all of her household are *doubly clothed* with scarlet." The point is obvious: the woman of the house has worked in such a way so as to provide her family with extra clothing for the winter cold.

But note that our verse begins by stating that she is "not afraid of the snow." She doesn't panic when the winter months come, because she has prepared for them. This speaks to her careful planning and disciplined use of her time. She not only concerns herself with the daily needs of her family, but looks ahead to see what needs they will have in the future, and prepares for them appropriately. As such, she rests assured that things are ready—she therefore offers an even greater benefit to her family, namely, the treasure of shalom.

22   *She makes coverings for herself; Her clothing is fine linen and purple.* One could hardly imagine, that, with all of the time that the virtuous woman spends caring for others, that she would have time to look after herself. But she does. After all, her actions flow from her strong, inner character. She knows who she is, and she dresses appropriately.

Her clothing is first described as "coverings" (מַרְבַדִּים), which means "coverings of tapestry." While she no doubt has her "work clothes," she nonetheless adorns herself with the beauty that bespeaks her inner worth. "Fine linen and purple" (שֵׁשׁ וְאַרְגָּמָן) describe the fabrics of the Ancient Near East that were most costly, and most sought after. Often royalty wore such garments, and we find *argaman* (purple) often woven with *teichelet* (deep blue) in the construction of the Tabernacle fabrics (Ex 25–39). So the language used here brings us an obvious picture: the woman of virtue is beautiful inside and out—her own clothes match the beauty of her inner character. This does not mean that only a woman with abundant financial means can achieve this kind of wardrobe. Remember, in our verse, she is making her own clothes. But what it does emphasize is that she takes care for how she looks. Any woman can dress beautifully if she takes care to do so.

23 *Her husband is known in the gates, When he sits among the elders of the land.* Coming as this does, after the verse extolling the beautiful garments of the wife, we should most likely understand that the husband's renown in the city gates (the place where the elders gather, and where the city's business district existed) is the result of her labors. Whether this relates to how he is dressed, or if it means that her reputation reflects on him, is not certain. But what is certain is that he is known as a man who has been fortunate enough to find such a wife. Rather than feeling the need to give excuses for the actions or appearance of his wife, he is rather praised by the other elders as one who is wealthy beyond what money can buy, for his wife is worth more than "fine jewels" (v. 10). The fact that he is able to put his trust in her has afforded him a shalom that is evident in all of his dealings. What is more, her reputation is added to his resumé.

24 *She makes linen garments and sells them, And supplies belts to the tradesmen.* The virtuous woman is industrious because her home labors produce more than the family needs. Her skills allow her to take what she has produced at home, and sell products to others. In this way, she contributes to the financial stability of the home as well.

  Here is a good example of a "cottage industry," in which a woman is able to gain financial advantage without leaving the domain of her primary responsibilities. Yet even in this, she finds a balance. Her home and family are not neglected in favor of producing goods for others. She is good at business—she knows how to make extra money in a skillful way, as the next verse emphasizes.

25   *Strength and dignity are her clothing, And she smiles at the future.* In the midst of emphasizing the woman's virtue in making garments, clothing her family, and adorning herself, one could over emphasize the outer beauty and thus diminish the inner character. Thus, the poetry moves to looking at clothing in a metaphorical way: she is not only clothed with tapestry and costly garments. She is also adorned with strength and dignity. She is not a shallow person who has simply "dressed up." Rather, her character and spiritual strength is just as evident as her outward apparel.

Because she is "clothed" with strength and dignity, "she smiles at the future." Literally, the Hebrew says, "she laughs at the final day." She is not constantly fretting about what tomorrow will bring. She has found contentment and shalom in the role she fulfills so well, because her strength of character has fit her for the present responsibilities. Thus, she entrusts the future to God. Her obedience today has built a fortress for tomorrow.

26   *She opens her mouth in wisdom, And the teaching of kindness is on her tongue.* The woman of valor is not some uneducated, unintellectual craftsman who works with her hands but not with her mind. On the contrary, her success as a homemaker, wife, and mother is grounded upon her wisdom. Thus, her words are valuable—they contain wisdom learned in the course of life, and from the study of Torah.

The Hebrew has "the Torah of kindness (תּוֹרַת־חֶסֶד) is on her tongue." Granted, "torah" means "teaching," so the normal English translation is accurate. However, *chesed* is also regularly used throughout the Tanach as a word associated with God's covenant faithfulness. We should just as well understand this verse as telling us that she is regularly engaged in the study of God's word, and that she therefore is a source of wisdom for all who are around her. Here we see once again that the spiritual strength of the virtuous woman is tied inevitably to her understanding and implementation of God's ways. Her decisions are based upon God's wisdom, and this is why she is successful.

27   *She looks well to the ways of her household, And does not eat the bread of idleness.* Literally, the Hebrew says: "she watches the ways

(הֲלִיכוֹת) of her household." This could be tied back to the previous verse, and her own study of the Torah. The *halakah*, the way the family "walks," is guarded by her watchful eye. She is diligent (not idle) in making sure that the home is a place were Torah is observed, and where the ways of God are the norm. While this surely does not negate the role of the husband in also leading the family in spiritual matters, it is clear that the wife has a major role to play in making Torah the foundation for the home. She does this in matters of food, clothing, schedules, and a host of other things. In short, she is intent upon making the home a place where the ways of Torah are constantly the focus for the household.

28   *Her children rise up and bless her; Her husband also, and he praises her, saying:* In the end, the greatest praise the woman of valor receives is from her own husband and children. Rather than being mocked or despised, her virtues are so evident that praise for her is the natural response. And here we learn an important lesson: the strong character and extolled virtues of the woman of valor must not be taken for granted. She deserves to be praised and encouraged on a regular basis. Once a husband has come to realize the immeasurable worth of a woman of valor, his praise for her will be public and often. The same is true of the children. Though in their immaturity they may take for granted the value of such a mother, as they see their father singing her praises, they too will join the chorus and recognize that the beauty of their home life is, in large measure, the results of her diligent labors.

29   *"Many daughters have done nobly, But you excel them all."* The praise of the virtuous woman is given here in a poetic line. Her virtue excels all others. Now obviously, if each household is making this statement, then we can only conclude (as we rightly should), that a virtuous woman, in her own home, is praised as the best. And why not? She alone can deal with her family as no one else can. She knows their needs, and she has committed herself to their care and success. In this regard, each woman of valor, in each home, excels all others.

30   *Charm is deceitful and beauty is vain, But a woman who fears the LORD, she shall be praised.* The Hebrew may give us a little different perspective. Literally it says: "Charm is a lie, and beauty is fleeting." In this regard, "charm" (חֵן) must be understood as an attempt to get what one wants by being "charming." The word יֵן, *chein,* "grace" or "favor" is generally used in a good sense in Proverbs. However, there is one place where it may be used negatively:

> Prov. 17:8 A bribe is a charm to the one who gives it; wherever he turns, he succeeds.

Here, a "charm" (חֵן) is connected with a bribe. In the same way, our text says that "charm is a lie." That is, putting on a front of kindness may win the day, but in the end will be seen for what it is—only a means to an end. The woman of virtue is not "charming" in this way. Rather, the gracious manner of her life is long-lasting, not something she can turn on when the moment requires it.

Likewise, "beauty" here should be understood as mere outward beauty without the corresponding inner depth of character. A woman who has only outward beauty will soon find that such beauty may fade in time. This is the meaning of הֶבֶל, translated "vain" in the English. The word means "a vapor" (as it does throughout Ecclesiastes). Now there is nothing wrong with a vapor, or the momentary pleasure a perfume may bring. But the point is that this is fleeting. Years may bring wrinkles, but the woman who has true inner beauty will remain truly beautiful throughout her life.

This is emphasized by the phrase "But a woman who fears Adonai, she shall be praised." The inner beauty of the woman of valor is grounded in her deep faith in the Almighty. This is what maintains her strength, gives her the desire to remain faithful, and supplies her with the skill and depth of character which enable her to have success in her womanly role of homemaker, wife, mother, and woman within the community.

31   *Give her the product of her hands, And let her works praise her in the gates.* Literally, the Hebrew says: "Give her the fruit of her hands." The idea of "giving" her the fruit of her hands means "acknowledge her for the work she has done, and for the results that have been achieved." This restates the praises of the husband and children in the previous verses. Her work is substantial, and the fruit of her work is eternal. She ought to be recognized for the high position she fills in the family and the community.

But even if there are those outside of the family who do not recognize her high value, and the supreme worth of her labors, that will not matter. In the long run, the fruit of her hands, which most likely refers to the lives of her children and husband, and the way they have been cared for by her, will find praise in the gates. Her reward is seen in the way she molds and affects the lives of others through her kind and careful labors at home.

Characteristics of a Godly Wife from the Apostolic Scriptures

We have looked briefly at a number of general characteristics given by way of example and clear teaching in the Tanach. It will also be helpful to overview some of the Apostolic teaching that touches on our subject.

One of the characteristics of a Godly husband, as we noted above, was that he is a provider for the family. This is derived from the general tenure of Scripture, but also from Paul's instructions to the older women of community (Tit 2:3–5):

> 3 Older women likewise are to be reverent in their behavior, not malicious gossips nor enslaved to much wine, teaching what is good, 4 so that they may encourage the young women to love their husbands, to love their children, 5 to be sensible, pure, workers at home, kind, being subject to their own husbands, so that the word of God will not be dishonored.

Here we find a general description of what Paul considers to be the basic role of the wife and mother: 1) they are to love their husbands, 2) they are to love their children, 3) they are to be sensible, 4) they are to be pure, 5) they are to be workers at home, 6) they are to be kind, and 7) they are to be subject to their own husbands. All of this has the effect of honoring the word of God. By this final statement in Paul's exhortation, we realize that the general list he gives us is not something new with him, but something that he understands to be in agreement with the Scriptures as a whole.

1. They are to love their husbands

At first reading, this may seem superfluous. Why would the Apostle emphasize at the beginning of his list, that wives should love their husbands? Would not this be a given? Yes, of course, it is! But when the Apostle begins with this, he is emphasizing that love is not primarily driven by feelings or circumstances, but by the determination of one's will. The translation "love their husbands" represents a single word in the

Greek: φίλανδρος, *philandros,* which means a woman who shows affection to her husband. The Greek word φίλος, *philos,* often carries the basic meaning of "friendship" or "having a special interest in someone." Thus Paul's admonition here is that wives should seek to be affectionate toward their husbands, nurturing a genuine friendship. Friendship is nurtured in the context of mutual respect, common interests, a desire to please each other, open communication, and a willingness to guard and care for each other. Learning to love your husband means growing in each of these areas.

2. *They are to love their children*

Again, we may, at first reading, think this goes without saying! But once again, Paul uses a single word to convey his meaning: φιλότεκνος, *philoteknos.* This is exactly the same kind of compound word that Paul used for "love their husbands." It means "be affectionate toward your children," or even, "be friendly to your children." The relationship between a mother and her children surely involves her being their authority, and Paul's exhortation here does not negate that, nor does it mean that mothers should try to just be "one of the gang" when it comes to her relationship with her children. Children do not need another "peer" in their mother—they need a mother! But the relationship between a mother and her children also partakes of all the goodness of friendship. This means that a relationship of trust, caring, communication and common interests are fostered within the context of the individual needs of each child. Or to put it another way: mothering should not be confined to a concept of duty. Surely there are duties, and these must be faithfully performed. But a Godly woman will find joy in her motherly responsibilities, a joy that comes from fostering genuine friendships with her children.

3. *They are to be sensible*

The word translated "sensible" is σώφρων, *sophron,* and is built on the word σώφια, *sophia,* "wisdom." A Godly wife and mother is one who grows in wisdom. This is also evidenced in the characteristic of self-control, and is the same word used of a qualification for an overseer (1Tim 3:2; Tit 1:8). A woman who is given to snap judgments and compulsive decisions will find her duties as a wife and mother greatly hampered.

Wisdom is the ability to take God's principles and regularly apply them to life's situations.

4. *They are to be pure*

The Greek word ἁγνος, *hagnos,* which is translated "pure" is used in the Lxx of the word of God, and of the Torah specifically:

> Ps 12:6 The oracles of the Lord are pure oracles; as silver tried in the fire, proved in a furnace of earth, purified seven times.
> Ps 19:9 The fear of the Lord is pure, enduring for ever and ever: the judgments of the Lord are true, and justified altogether.

In both of these examples (and in many others), the word has the sense of something that is not a mixture. As silver refined in the fire, and thus is pure of any dross, so the oracles of the Lord are pure.

Paul's sense here is most likely that a Godly wife and mother is not divided in her life—she is single-hearted. She does not see her position in the home as just one aspect of her life, with many other things dividing her energies, goals, and perspective. Like the woman of valor, she is engaged in a myriad of enterprises, and she is skillful, talented, and creative. Yet her life is bound up with husband and family, and she wants it that way. She does not feel "trapped" into serving her family while her true desires are elsewhere. She is pure in heart, having received her role as wife and mother as a blessing from the Almighty.

5. *They are to be workers at home*

Once again, Paul uses a single word to denote this characteristic: οἰκουργός, *oikourgos,* which is a compound word made up of *oikos,* "house" and *ergos,* "work." We might translate it "homemaker." Others have translated the word "busy at home." For Paul, the norm was that wives and mothers should find their days filled with the high and happy responsibilities of making the home a place where a family can be nurtured, and pouring her life into the lives of her family. Surely a Godly wife and mother has friendships and activities outside of the home. But what Paul teaches here is that her primary life work—her over arching role in life, relates to her home and family.

What does this say for women working outside of the home as a wage earner for the family? Obviously, there are times when this cannot be avoided, especially for single mothers. But in our society, the desire for affluence has eclipsed the needs of the family. Mothers that work so that the family can be in a higher income bracket should consider the trade-offs. Regardless of what one may think, a family is far better off with Mom at home than with all the things and comforts an extra paycheck might afford.

6. *They are to be kind*

Actually, the word Paul uses here is a common word for "good" (ἀγαθός, *agathos*), which speaks of "meeting a high standard of worth and merit." As a woman fulfills her role of wife, mother, and homemaker, she achieves a high standard of worth and merit, not only in the eyes of her family and community, but also before her Maker.

7. *They are to be subject to their own husbands*

The Apostolic Scriptures consistently admonish wives to be in submission to their husbands:

> Eph. 5:22 Wives, be subject to your own husbands, as to the Lord.
> Eph. 5:24 But as the *kehilah* is subject to Messiah, so also the wives ought to be to their husbands in everything.
> Col. 3:18 Wives, be subject to your husbands, as is fitting in the Lord.
> 1Pet. 3:1 In the same way, you wives, be submissive to your own husbands so that even if any of them are disobedient to the word, they may be won without a word by the behavior of their wives,
> 1Pet. 3:5 For in this way in former times the holy women also, who hoped in God, used to adorn themselves, being submissive to their own husbands;

It is understandable why this characteristic of a Godly wife has not always been so readily nor easily received. Let's face it, submission to anyone is not an issue until there's a problem or disagreement. In any situation, as long as one is content with the situation, it is not difficult to submit to the authority of those over us. It is when an authority asks us to do something we really would rather not do, or makes a decision that goes against what we want—then the issue of submission to authority becomes a factor.

We may make a few preliminary observations relating to this whole matter of a wife's submission to her husband. First, it is often overlooked that no where in the Apostolic Scriptures is there even a hint that it is the duty of a husband to make his wife submit to him. In all of the places where the wife is admonished to submit to her husband, the admonition is directed to her, not to the husband. This is important because it emphasizes that submission is the function of the wife's will, not something into which she is forced or coerced. Indeed, forced submission (we might better call it subjugation) is not true submission at all. Compliance while grinding teeth and *kvetching* is also not submission. What the Scriptures enjoin upon the wife is a willing submission to her husband *because she knows that this is what God wants, and she trusts that He will bless her and her family as she follows His will.*

Secondly, love is never without submission. For this reason, the whole matter of submission is a mutual reality in any good marriage. What I mean by this is that when a husband loves his wife, he is constantly engaged in submitting his will, his desires, his time, his energies, and of course, his pocketbook to her needs. As he submits to God, he puts her needs before himself. That means he is living a life of submission, often foregoing his own desires in order to meet the needs and desires of his wife. The best example of this is Yeshua: as He submitted to the Father, He went to the cross for His bride. So submission is not something in which the wife alone engages. In a loving relationship, there is always a sense of mutual submission.

Yet thirdly, when push-comes-to-shove, the final responsibility for decision-making and leadership falls on the shoulders of the husband, and the wife is called to submit to his decisions. If the husband has acted with respect and care toward his wife, and if the wife has evidenced a willingness to submit to him, even these times will not be burdensome. It is when we neglect to act in love—to put the other as more important than ourselves—that both leading and submitting becomes a wearisome burden.

The Greek word for "be subject" or "to submit" is instructive in itself. It is ὑποτάσσω It is the very dwelling of God with the believer that is the connection to our Apostolic reading:, *hupotasso,* which is made up of the word *hupo,* "under" and *tasso,* "to put in order." Submission is the willingness to follow a prescribed order, in which one puts oneself under the leadership of another and willingly follows. This is what God expects of a wife, that she willingly follows the leadership of her husband.

This does not mean, of course, that God expects a wife to remain in submission to an abusive husband, or to simply accept an ungodly or immoral environment which a husband may create out of his own way-wardness. In such situations it is required of a wife that she speak up, and let her husband know that such behavior is unacceptable, and that it will not be tolerated. But barring these exceptional situations, the role of the Godly wife is one of submission to her husband.

Note that the Titus text we are considering emphasizes that a wife be subject "to her *own* husband." She is not required to act in the same submission to other men as she does toward her husband. This is because such a role of submission is not a matter of gender (as though all women are to submit to all men), but submission to one's husband is a matter of the marriage covenant into which they have entered. The submission of a wife to her husband is to be a dramatic picture of the community's sub-mission to Yeshua (Eph 5:32), and thus the one-to-one submission rela-tionship fits the picture.

It is easy to see that when a husband is not fulfilling his role of humble and careful leadership, or when a wife has turned inward and is intent upon pleasing herself rather than serving her family, such a scenario has all the ingredients for disaster. As a husband comes to believe that the best way to bring his wife into submission is to exert his authority and rule with a heavy hand, the wife naturally resists such tactics and becomes more resolute in her unwillingness to follow him. As she resists his au-thority, he becomes more heavy handed, and the cycle spirals downward. If something doesn't change, one of two things occurs: either the marriage fails and they separate or divorce, or they grow apart from each other, trying to find satisfaction in their separate lives, since they discover that when they're "doing their own thing," they don't have to deal with their embattled relationship. I've known couples who were married for 25 years with separate bedrooms at opposite ends of the house! Neither of these scenarios is acceptable. But how to stop the downward spiral often eludes us.

In fact, the way to overcome the demise of relationship as outlined above is just opposite of what we might naturally think. A husband will not bring his wife into submission by ratcheting up his voice of author-ity. Rather, when he willingly serves her, submitting his own desires and will to meet her needs, he will discover that her response to him is more and more one of submission. Likewise, a wife who increasingly resists her husband's heavy handed authority will discover that submitting to him will often change his ways.

But that's not our natural way of thinking. A husband reasons that if he stops reminding everyone of his authority, and instead humbly serves his wife, attempting to meet her needs, he'll just be taken advantage of. "If I give into her and serve her rather than ruling over her, she'll just take advantage of me and the whole situation will be worse than ever!" The natural tendency of the wife is to think that if she submits to her husband, he'll just control her all the more, and her life will be like an indentured slave. "I do enough for him anyway! If I give into him and tell him I'm willing to follow his lead, he'll just take advantage of me! I'll never get anything I want!"

God's ways are not our ways, and His thoughts are not our thoughts. But when we conform to His ways, we find that they work. A husband who serves his wife will find in her someone eager to submit to his leadership. And a wife who willing and lovingly supports and submits to her husband will find in him a man who will work hard to support, protect, and nurture her.

I recognize that I'm speaking in broad strokes here, and that there are exceptions to the rule. But the exceptions do not overturn the rule. In general, a man wants a wife who respects him, supports him, and follows his lead. And a woman is looking for a husband who will support, protect, and nurture her. When a husband and wife follow God's way in the marriage relationship, they find in each other exactly what each one desires.

The best illustration of this is Yeshua, and His relationship to His bride, the *kehilah* of believers that confess Him to be Master and Savior. Paul casts this relationship between Yeshua and His people in the metaphor of a marriage:

> Eph. 5:25 Husbands, love your wives, just as Messiah also loved *His kehilah* and gave Himself up for her, 26 so that He might sanctify her, having cleansed her by the washing of water with the word, 27 that He might present to Himself *His kehilah* in all her glory, having no spot or wrinkle or any such thing; but that she would be holy and blameless. 28 So husbands ought also to love their own wives as their own bodies. He who loves his own wife loves himself; 29 for no one ever hated his own flesh, but nourishes and cherishes it, just as Messiah also does *His kehilah*, 30 because we are members of His body. 31 For this reason a man shall leave his father and mother and shall be joined to his wife, and the two shall become one flesh. 32 This mystery is great; but I am speaking with reference to Messiah and *His kehilah*. 33 Nevertheless, each individual among you also is to love his own wife even as himself, and the wife must see to it that she respects her husband.

From this key passage we may note a number of important things:

1. The love that a husband has for his wife is seen in the way he gives himself for her. That means giving up one's own life (wants, desires, time, money, energies, etc.) for the sake of his wife.
2. When a husband gives up his life for the sake of his wife, he changes her—he helps her fulfill the role for which she was created.
3. As the wife submits to the self-sacrifice of her husband, she attains to the honor and glory for which she was created.
4. As a husband loves and nourishes his wife with the same tenacity that he would care for himself, he finds his wife responding to his love.
5. This is exactly how we who are believers respond to Yeshua. Because He was willing to lay down His life for us, we are eager to show Him our appreciation, and to follow His leading. We love Him, because He first loved us.
6. It is never difficult to submit to someone who has demonstrated that he is willing to do whatever is needed to meet our needs!

Summary

In this chapter, we have given a brief overview of the characteristics of a Godly wife as the Scriptures portray them. From the example of Rivka, Prov 31, and Titus 2, we saw:

1. Spiritual strength: a willingness to trust that God is in control, and to grow in trust and faith in Him. She fears the Lord, and studies to know His will and ways.
2. Beauty: both inward and outward.
3. Respect: a husband will respond in wonderful ways toward a wife who lets him know, in word and deed, that she respects him, that she is for him, and that she will do all in her power to help him succeed. She willingly submits to his leadership.
4. Doer of good: a Godly wife seeks to enhance the lives of her husband and family.
5. Hard worker: she is diligent in her tasks of making the home a

place where the family can be nurtured, and where there is a refuge of shalom. She learns to be skillful in these tasks. She is not lazy.

6. Creative: she is not content with mediocrity. Her creativity enhances the home and gives advantages to her family.

7. Wise: she applies God's teaching (Torah) to the practical aspects of life, both for herself and her family.

8. Strength: in her dependence upon God, she finds an inner strength needed to accomplish her tasks.

9. Generous: she is willing to help those less fortunate.

10. Love: she has committed herself to loving her husband and her children as the top priority in her life.

Let's Talk About It!

1. How has the feminist movement in our times undermined the family? How has it changed what we define as "feminine?"

2. What are some of the subtle "givens" of the feminist movement in our times which have become common even in the thinking of many evangelical Christians?

3. Consider some of the current movies or TV programs that are popular. In general, how do these portray the role of women? Discuss how the media of our day has affected the basic roles of wife and husband.

4. Considering the description of the Woman of Valor (Prov 31), which characteristics do you think are most difficult to attain?

5. Discuss why it is sometimes difficult for a wife to submit to her husband. From a woman's standpoint, what could a husband do to make submission to his leadership easier? What specific areas are the most difficult in terms of submitting to your husband?

6. Discuss the issue of a husband and wife who are still raising children, and the wife is employed outside of the home. What are the trade-offs in such a scenario?

7. What about a woman being the "bread-winner," and the Dad staying home with the children? What family dynamics does this change?

Chapter 7
Betrothal & Marriage

As we have seen, the relationship of marriage is a gift of the Creator. As such, it is sacred. It rightly exists within the boundaries in which it was given, and outside of these boundaries, is not valid. From the beginning, the relationship of husband and wife was prescribed by God Himself (Gen 2:24) as the uniting of a man and woman to form a union separate from, or in addition to, their respective families. Cast in the terms of a covenant, marriage therefore was given legal as well as societal sanctions. It involved not only the matter of rightful ownership of material goods, but also of the authority that is vested within the newly formed family. The man and the woman who are united in marriage leave the direct authority structure of their parents, and forge a separate family with its own responsibilities and authority.

It is therefore required of parents that they prepare their children for marriage. This preparation involves both guarding and training. Parents must envision for each of their children the time when, if God wills, they will marry. This means that as we raise our children, we will have in mind the necessary character qualities and beliefs that they must have in order to honor God as a husband or wife. Our primary concern is not to prepare them for a career or even for other societal roles (as important as these may be), but to make them ready to be a Godly spouse and to carry on the role of a Godly parent.

This preparation of our children likewise involves guarding them, and all the more so as they approach the time when they will marry. But the ability to guard them from wrong relationships, and from those things that would take them in the wrong direction, is based upon the relationship we have fostered with them throughout their lives. A return to a biblical perspective of betrothal and marriage will only work if our relationship with our children has grown deep over the years. This is because in guarding them, we may need to restrict them from things that, in the emotions of their youth, may seem "unfair" and "unnecessary." Yet if a strong relationship of love and trust has been established, they will be able to submit to the leadership of their parents in the very important matter of relationships.

The Father as Guardian

In the Scriptures, the role of training and guarding children is surely the responsibility of both parents. The Proverbs exhort children to value the instruction of father and mother, and even give strong warning to children who might despise their parents:

> Prov. 6:20 My son, observe the commandment of your father and do not forsake the teaching of your mother;

> Prov. 23:25 Let your father and your mother be glad, and let her rejoice who gave birth to you.

> Prov. 30:17 The eye that mocks a father and scorns a mother, the ravens of the valley will pick it out, and the young eagles will eat it.

Yet there is a clear priority of responsibility given to the father. For instance, in Num 30, a husband may annul a vow made by his wife, and a father may do likewise for a vow made by his daughter. Here we see a particular responsibility of a father in guarding his daughter. Interestingly, there is nothing about a father annulling a vow of his son. From the Torah's perspective, an adult son still living at home is responsible for his own vows, apparently because he is being treated as one who would eventually be responsible to guard his own family.

This same emphasis may be seen in the laws given in Deut 22:

> 13 "If any man takes a wife and goes in to her and then turns against her, 14 and charges her with shameful deeds and publicly defames her, and says, 'I took this woman, but when I came near her, I did not find her a virgin,' 15 then the girl's father and her mother shall take and bring out the evidence of the girl's virginity to the elders of the city at the gate. 16 "The girl's father shall say to the elders, 'I gave my daughter to this man for a wife, but he turned against her; 17 and behold, he has charged her with shameful deeds, saying, "I did not find your daughter a virgin." But this is the evidence of my daughter's virginity.' And they shall spread the garment before the elders of the city. 18 "So the elders of that city shall take the man and chastise him, 19 and they shall fine him a hundred shekels of silver and give it to the girl's father, because he publicly defamed a virgin of Israel. And she shall remain his wife; he cannot divorce her all his days. 20 "But if this charge is true, that the girl was not found a virgin, 21 then they shall bring out the girl to the doorway of her father's

> house, and the men of her city shall stone her to death because she has
> committed an act of folly in Israel by playing the harlot in her father's
> house; thus you shall purge the evil from among you.

Beyond the fact that this text clearly marks pre-marital sex as an evil, a number of important issues arise from this passage. First, we should remember that in the Torah, capital punishment for sexual sins pertains to adultery and harlotry. In Ex 22:16–17, for example, pre-marital sexual relations incur a penalty, but not death. Thus, in the case represented in Deut 22, the issue is that a woman who fraudulently presents herself as a virgin, and then is later found to have had sexual relations, has put herself in the same class as a prostitute. She has lied about her past, and cannot be trusted truthfully to disclose the extent of her promiscuity. As such, she is presumed to have engaged in harlotry.

But secondly, note that throughout the ordeal, the father of the girl is the one who represents her in legal matters. Her legal status is in his hands because her sexual purity is his responsibility. And if she is found to be guilty of the charge, she is not executed in the field, or in some judicial court, but "in the doorway of her father's house." This makes it clear that her sexual sin was only secondarily against her newly married husband. It was *primarily* against her father whose responsibility it was to guard and keep her.

We may also note Ex 22:16–17

> "If a man seduces a virgin who is not engaged, and lies with her, he must
> pay a dowry for her to be his wife. If her father absolutely refuses to give
> her to him, he shall pay money equal to the dowry for virgins.

Here, once again, the final decision is in the hands of the father. If he decides that his daughter is not to marry the man with whom she has had relations, then no marriage is forthcoming. Yet the man is still required to pay the fine equal to what the dowry would have been had he been allowed to marry. And presumably he pays the dowry to the girl's father.

The primary responsibility of the father to guard his daughter is likewise seen in the fact that in the Gospels, the phrase "marry and given in marriage" is customary to describe marriage itself (Matt. 22:30; Mark 12:25; Luke 17:27; 20:34-35). Here "marry" most likely refers to the man, and "given in marriage" to the woman. The woman is guarded in the home of her father until such time as he relinquishes his authority over her by "giving" her to the man she will marry. In this way, she moves from the guardianship of her father to that of her husband.

This is not to suggest that a woman is morally inferior, or that apart from the protection of a father or husband, she would inevitably fail. Examples abound of widows and single women who have demonstrated strong faith and moral character. But it is clear that God has designed women to be protected, and this protection begins with a father, and is transferred to a husband at the time of marriage. While this goes counter to our own society and culture, it is nonetheless God's design, and we do well to adhere to it. The reality is that women who are afforded loving and careful protection find in such protection a place of strength in which they flourish and fulfill their God-given role to its fullness.

But we may wonder why the Scriptures consistently portray the father as guardian of his daughter and not his son. It surely is not that he feels any less responsibility or love toward his son. Rather, it is based upon a very practical reality: the daughter is more vulnerable to the approaches of men. Thus, since every father must guard his daughter, no marriage can be arranged without the direct involvement of a father. From God's perspective, when daughters are protected, marriage is likewise protected.

Why Dating is Not God's Design

Having emphasized the role of a father in protecting his daughter, it becomes evident why the modern phenomenon of dating does not work. First, in our modern times, young couples would never think of having the girl's father come along on dates! Yet when a young girl leaves the home on a date, the father has no ability to maintain his responsibility as her guardian. He has allowed his daughter to enter an emotional, momentary relationship in which immaturity and sensual lust have no checks. Rather than guarding her, he has allowed her to be in a place where she is vulnerable not only to her own weaknesses, but to the desires of a young man who may or may not have the disciplines of moral character.

Secondly, dating is not God's design because it does not have marriage as its goal. Dating is a social activity in which boys and girls practice short-term relationships that go beyond mere acquaintance. There are the expectations of exclusivity, physical and emotional expressions of love, and social status. Yet none of these are presumed to lead to marriage. As such, young people learn the devastating "art" of "falling in love," being hurt, breaking up, and starting all over again. The dating scene revolves almost entirely around physical attractions, and teaches all of the wrong messages, primarily, that relationships of the deepest nature are usually temporary, and that after one has "healed" from the trauma of being rejected, there is always another relationship to take its place. In short, dating trains our young people for divorce.

Thirdly, dating promotes a separation from the parents. Even in the "best case scenario," where young people have a healthy respect for their parents, and have fostered good relationships with them, dating is viewed as a private experience in which the young people are away from home, and "on their own." Rather than drawing upon the wisdom of their parents and family, dating gives the false impression that young people have the ability to make their own decisions about a future spouse. In this way, dating is sort of like window shopping. They figure that if they date enough, they'll finally find the one that "fits." The whole idea that one's parents have wisdom and particular insights into their children's character and needs is mostly undermined by the cultural phenomenon of dating.

It is no wonder, then, that in our times, pre-martial sex has become the norm, and "living together" apart from marriage is accepted as almost normative. Since divorce is more common than not, the temporary arrangement taught in dating has become "safer" than a life-long commitment. And this is not simply the case in the "world," but it continues to become the norm among many religious communities as well.

When we honestly consider the message that dating gives to our children; when we realize that in allowing our children to date, we have put them in an unguarded place of vulnerability, and that we are teaching them all the wrong messages about what marriage really is, we are left with the question of how we are to go about securing a life-long mate for our children. The modern phenomenon of dating has so eclipsed our culture that we wonder if there are any viable alternatives. In fact, we know that there is, but we wonder again if our children will be mature enough to recognize that the way of courtship and betrothal offers a far greater advantage. For Torah communities, this presents one of our greatest challenges—to return to a biblical model of marriage, and to help our young people recover the means by which they too will find the lasting, joyful relationship of marriage.

In facing this challenge, we are met with having to learn for ourselves what courtship is, and how it should work. Most of us never experience it for ourselves. Admittedly, most of us entered marriage after years of dating, and thus we begin as learners in an area that, generations ago, would have been the norm.

Betrothal in the Scriptures and in History

The Hebrew Scriptures regularly present the picture of a pre-marriage arrangement called "engagement" or "betrothal" (Ex. 22:15; Deut. 20:7; 22:23, 25, 27-28; 28:30; 2Sam. 3:14; Hos. 2:21-22). The Hebrew word used in each of these instances is אָרַשׂ, *'eras.* The word itself may have a root meaning of "desire," "request," "ask," or "inquire" (based upon the Akkadian root *ereshu*), but the word became a technical term for acquiring a wife. It appears to have involved the payment of the bride price, which legally bound the man and woman for future marriage. For this reason, the rape of a betrothed woman required capital punishment for the assailant (Deut 22:13f).

It would also seem that in ancient Israel (and this was surely true in later rabbinic legislation) the betrothal was what gave legitimacy to the marriage. Without a valid betrothal, there could not be a valid marriage. In the Deut passages listed above, a man who was betrothed to a woman was exempt from military service in war. Whereas in other Ancient Near Eastern cultures the exemption was most likely one based upon superstition (because a betrothed man was thought of as particularly vulnerable to influences of magic and demonic forces), in Israel, the basis for military exemption was humanitarian. The important aspects of normative family life took precedence over the requirements of the army.

Betrothal also is used metaphorically of God's relationship to Israel. Hosea portrays a time when Israel would be faithful to God as His betrothed wife:

> Hos. 2:19 "I will betroth you to Me forever; Yes, I will betroth you to Me in righteousness and in justice, in lovingkindness and in compassion, 20 and I will betroth you to Me in faithfulness. Then you will know the LORD.

Whereas Israel had acted in unfaithfulness to her betrothed One, He would cleanse her, and once again pay the betrothal price to secure her as His wife.

Yet the Tanach never outlines exactly how betrothal was achieved (except for payment of a bride price to the father). The method, ceremony, length of the betrothal period, and other details are never clearly spelled out. For these we are left to consult the history of betrothal among the Jewish communities of late antiquity.

Betrothal in the Rabbinic Literature

In rabbinic terms, betrothal is known as שִׁידּוּכִין, *shiduchin,* meaning "settlements" or "negotiations." *Shiduchin* is defined as "the mutual promise between a man and a woman to contract a marriage at some future time and the formulations of the terms (called *tena'im*) on which it shall take place" (*Ency Jud* 4:753). The Sages describe a marriage (*kidushin*) without prior *shiduchin* as licentiousness and prescribed that "he who enters into a marriage without *shiduchin* is liable to be flogged" (b.*Kidushin*12b). Moreover, when a couple enters *shiduchin,* their personal status is not changed, meaning that one cannot require of the other some special performance, since the marriage is not yet consummated, and since a basic aspect of marriage from a rabbinic standpoint is free and mutual consent of each party. Yet *shiduchin* is legally binding, and dissolving the betrothal status may result in payment of penalty, return of gifts, and compensation for debts that may have been incurred in preparation of the wedding itself.

The enactment of betrothal was accompanied by a public festive meal, in which family and guests were invited. This took place in the house of the bride's father where she remained following the ceremony. In fact, the procession of the bride to the house of her groom was a primary aspect of the wedding day itself. Until the wedding, however, the bride remained in the house of her father. The ceremony of the betrothal involved the simple statement of the groom to the bride: "Today you are betrothed to me according to the law of Moses and Israel" (t.*Ketubot* 4:9). The symbolic payment of money was given to the bride's father. Shammai held that the minimum was one *dinar,* but Hillel held that even a *perutah* would suffice (m.*Kidushin* 1:1). One source notes that some who lived in the Land were accustomed to betroth their wives with rings, in contrast to the practice of Babylonian Jews (see "Home & Family" in Safrai, et al, *The Jewish People in the First Century*, 2:756).

The betrothal ceremony was usually held in the evening, and blessings were pronounced over the couple in the presence of ten men. It was also customary for the groom to present his future bride with the *ketubbah* which enumerated in detail his responsibilities toward her and stipulated a sum of not less than two hundred *dinars* which he agreed that she should receive in the event of divorce or his death.[1]

The exact length of the betrothal period is not prescribed, though the Mishnah records that "a virgin is granted twelve months to provide for herself; and like as such time is granted to the woman, so is it granted to the man to provide for himself" (m.*Ketubot* 1.5; t.*Ketubot* 1.4). During the betrothal period, it was customary for the groom to send gifts to his bride-to-be as well as to her family. He might also give her gifts at other times, and these would be her possession (not her families) so that she would bring them with her when she moved to the house of her husband.

The financial arrangements for the wedding feast itself, and for the physical aspects of the wedding ceremony, were the responsibility of the groom and his family. The bride provided only for her own adornments and clothes. There was also the custom, however, of an institution called *shushbinut*, which was an organization of men who covenanted with each other that when any member or a son of a member married, each of the others would contribute a sum of money to meet the expenses. Such an institution resulted in close friendships among the *shushbinut*, and as such they often took leading roles in the wedding ceremony itself.

Virgin brides were usually married on Wednesdays, and widows on Thursdays, a custom that disappeared under the religious persecutions of Hadrian (m.*Ketubot* 1.1; t.*Ketubot* 1.1). The wedding celebration itself consisted of preparing the bride in her home, carrying the bride from her home to that of the groom on a decorated carriage carried through the streets of the city, accompanied by song, dance, musical instruments, and applause (m.*Ketubot* 2:1; m.*Sota* 9:14). Likewise, since the procession was usually toward evening, friends of the bride would proceed the carriage with lamps or candles. So important was the wedding procession that the Sages encouraged students of the Torah to interrupt their studies to join the procession (b.*Ketubot* 17a). Once the procession arrived at the home of the groom, he would go out to meet her and bring her into his home. The *chuppah* was most likely in the courtyard of the groom's home.

---

1   If divorce occurred as a result of the wife's misconduct, the payment promised in the *ketubbah* was not required.

In later times, the *chuppah* itself functioned symbolically as the groom's dwelling place.

In later times of persecution, the separation of the *shiduchin* ceremony from the actual wedding ceremony (*Kidushin*) was discontinued, and the two ceremonies melded into one at the time of the wedding. This was because once it was known publicly that a Jewish woman was betrothed, she became highly vulnerable to misuse by the prevailing government officials. Thus, in the later centuries, the formal declaration of betrothal ("Today you are betrothed to me according to the Law of Moses and of Israel") was included in the wedding ceremony under the *chuppah*, and the *ketubbah* was signed and delivered at the wedding ceremony as well.

It is not difficult to see how the ancient traditions of the Jewish wedding are represented in many Christian weddings of our times. The engagement with a ring that proceeds the actual wedding, the procession of the bride to the groom who awaits at the front of the auditorium, the groomsmen and bridesmaids, the vows that are taken, the signing of certificates, and carrying of the bride over the threshold of the groom's home, etc., all find their origins in the ancient Hebrew wedding.

In the rabbinic *halachah*, there are provisions for breach of the betrothal contract, such as a change of status which would make either of the parties incapable of fulfilling their promised obligations, or other matters that the court might find valid, as when a parent may agree to the terms of the betrothal without their child's knowledge, but then the child refuses to accept the arrangement. In the event of a valid defense for dissolving the *shiduchin,* no liability is incurred. However, if there is a breach of the *shiduchin* without valid defense, the sum required for payment as prescribed in the *ketubbah* is to be paid by the offending party. Further compensation may be sought for debts incurred in preparation for the wedding, or for other related debts. Gifts given at the *shiduchin* ceremony are to be returned, regardless who gave them, including one's own family.

From this very brief overview of betrothal in the Scriptures and from Rabbinic sources, we may highlight the following significant aspects:

1. The betrothal was made voluntarily between a man and woman, but with the agreement of the woman's father.
2. The betrothal was a public ceremony, which therefore publicly set the man and woman apart for each other, anticipating a future date

at which time they would be married.

3. The woman remained in her father's home until the date of the wedding, at which time she was transferred to the home of her husband where the wedding ceremony took place.

4. The betrothal was legally binding, so that to fail to follow through in marriage required a public dissolution of the betrothal before a court of judges. Damages could be sought by the innocent party for the breach of the betrothal contract.

5. The exact betrothal period is not prescribed, though a minimum of 12 months is stated as preparation time for both the groom and the bride if they so desire. It would appear that among other things, the betrothal period allowed time for the couple to gather the necessary things and finances needed to establish their own home.

6. A valid marriage required a valid betrothal. Marriage without betrothal (in a case where betrothal would have been valid) was deemed valid, though licentious. The norm was public betrothal followed by a public wedding

Courtship: Preparing our Children for Marriage

We have already seen that biblically, it is the father's responsibility to guard his daughter. This means that he also has the authority to guard his daughter's romantic expressions. From the beginning, God made man and woman to be together, so it is no wonder that He created us with a need and desire for each other. That is normal. In fact, when there is no desire for the opposite sex, there is a problem. Various factors could contribute to such a scenario, but clearly it is not normal: God created us for each other. We should expect, then, that as our children grow and mature, they will naturally be considering who might become their life-long companion in marriage. Daughters, especially, will spend plenty of time dreaming about "Mr. Right"—what he will be like, how he will act, what he will look like, and all of the rest. There's nothing wrong with this—in fact, there's everything right with this. Such thoughts are the natural outworking of how God fashioned us. And of course, sons will also have in mind the kind of young lady to whom he is attracted. Again, this is what God expects.

The problem we have, however, is that in our world, the feelings of romance have entirely eclipsed the whole issue of male/female relationships. As we noted earlier, this is obviously strengthened by recreational dating. How one "feels" about another person is generally what drives the male/female relationship in our society. And when feelings change, so does the relationship.

This does not mean that romantic feelings are wrong! On the contrary, romance is a gift from God Himself, enwrapping two lives together in the joy of deep companionship. But if we were to use the analogy of a house, romance would be the equivalent of interior decorating, not the construction of the foundation. A house that may be lavishly decorated but has no structural integrity, is destroyed in the first big storm. The same is true of marriages that are based on romantic attraction only—the first time trouble comes, they very often fall apart.

So it is the responsibility of fathers to guard the romantic feelings of their daughters. As important as these feelings are, they are ill-fit for the kind of objective judgments that need to be made when it comes to choosing a husband.

Preparing Sons

Genesis 2:24 teaches that a son *leaves* his father and mother and cleaves to his wife. This means that the son becomes a guardian himself: first of his wife, and then of daughters as the Lord gives them children. In order to be a guardian of others, sons must be instructed in God's pattern of marriage. This means that sons must understand that marriage is defined by God, and that the boundaries given by God are what constitute rightful marriage. The Torah has specific instructions about whom one can marry and those who are forbidden. Leviticus 18 outlines those who, being too close in bloodline, are forbidden to marry. When John the Immerser confronted Herod about marrying his brother's wife (Matt 14:4), he said: "It is not lawful for you to have her." This demonstrates that a magistrate or a government official cannot redefine marriage for us. God's definition and parameters for marriage remain constant throughout time. Thus, it is important for our sons to know how God defines marriage, and what He has said is lawful and what is not. In a time when marriage is constantly being redefined against the norms of Scripture, it is all the more important that our sons understand God's instructions for marriage.

This pertains to the issue of divorce. A person who is granted a divorce from the civil courts may or may not be divorced in God's eyes.

Entering marriage with someone who claims to be following God's ways, but who has separated from her husband unlawfully, can only bring trouble.

The Scriptures also teach us that believers in Yeshua should marry a believer, not an unbeliever. Paul writes in 1Cor 7:39,

> A wife is bound as long as her husband lives; but if her husband is dead, she is free to be married to whom she wishes, only in the Lord.

Marrying "in the Lord" means that a believer is to be joined to another believer, because a believer is not his own—he or she has been purchased by Yeshua, and belongs to Him. Becoming one with an unbeliever is therefore out of the question.

We may note several other things from this verse. First, marriage is for life. Our sons need to know this both from our teaching them and from our example of faithfulness in our own marriages. Marriage is a life-long commitment—only the death of one's spouse frees one to marry another. Granted, in some circumstances (sexual infidelity; abandonment by an unbelieving spouse; physical abuse [?]) God grants a rightful divorce and thus the privilege of remarriage. Yet one should never enter marriage unless one is fully committed to a life-long faithfulness to their spouse. This is God's norm for marriage (cf. Matt 19:6), because (let us remember), God intends marriage to be a living manifestation of His own fidelity to His covenant people.

One other thing from this verse (1Cor 7:39) that is worthy of note in our discussion: a woman who is married, and whose husband dies, is free to marry "whom she wishes." This tells us that a widow is not required to return to her father's house, and come under his guardianship, though of course, this would always be an option, and in many cases (especially if she is younger) might be the best option. Still, having transferred her allegiance to her husband, she is now free to marry according to her own discretion. Of course, wisdom is found in the multitude of counsel, and any woman of valor would seek much advice in such a situation.

Most importantly, a son should be taught that marriage is a covenantal relationship, not a metaphysical one. That means that he needs to learn the value of commitment to what is true rather than to what he feels. Teaching our sons to make decisions based upon what is right rather than on what is expedient is an all-important ingredient in preparing them for marriage. Teaching the *mitzvot* is therefore the preparation for marriage, for we obey God, first and foremost, because it is the right thing to do, whether we feel like it or not. What may appear as small things are actually the training for greater things in life. When a son learns to say "no" to forbidden foods, for instance, even when doing so makes him look conspicuous or "out of sync" with the others, this prepares him to make the right decisions in matters far more important. Another example: a personal commitment to honoring the Sabbath because that is what God has commanded, trains him to honor the commitment of his marriage, because that is also what God has commanded. In short, Torah living is the school that teaches our children about life as a covenant commitment. It prepares them for the covenant of marriage.

Our sons also need to learn the role of being leaders. Leadership takes on all manner of modes. Some will be leaders of many, while others will be leaders of few. And the general personalities and giftedness with which our sons are endowed will determine the range of their leadership responsibilities. But regardless of the extent of their leadership roles, the same principles apply. That means we must constantly give our sons more and more responsibilities as they grow into maturity. The ability to make decisions and lead is something that is cultivated and enhanced through experience. A man who makes snap decisions or (on the other end of the scale) is frozen every time he is called upon to bear the responsibilities of a decision, will not be the husband he is called to be. Leadership means being able to weigh the various factors in a given scenario, and decide what direction to go, based upon known principles. That means that our sons need to know God's word—the place where God's enduring principles are revealed. It also means that as leaders within their homes, they must have learned to cultivate their own spiritual relationship with God, for it is from the spiritual strength they gain from their own walk with the Almighty that they will grow in wisdom and ability to lead their wife and family.

That means our sons need to learn to be men. They need to understand what it is to be masculine. In a society where gender distinctions are constantly eroded, we must work all that much harder to help our sons appreciate their masculinity. That means we have to put our sons in situations where they might fail—where they are called upon to go beyond what they might normally think they can do. For example, let your son change the flat tire (with supervision, of course). Let him get his hands dirty changing the oil, or replacing the spark plugs. Work together on home repairs. Once you've showed him how to accomplish a given task, hand him the tools and let him do it himself. If home repairs are not your *forte,* then find other activities that you can work on together, that will call upon your son to "stretch himself." But our sons must also learn that being a gentleman is a significant part of being masculine. The macho presentation of masculinity, so often portrayed in the media, is a wimpy representation at best. True men know how to be gentlemen. Their strength lies not only in their willingness to get the job done, but also in their ability to treat others with genuine respect.

We must also teach our sons the real story about sexual desires. These are God-given, which is why we naturally desire to "cleave" to our wife. But these desires will be misused if they are fulfilled outside of marriage. So we need to talk directly to our sons to tell them that their sexual hunger is normal, but that natural "hunger" cannot be satisfied until they get married. We need to warn our sons about the dangers of pornography and let them know that it is a mental poison that ruins the soul. In a society where morality has declined to an almost nonexistent level, pornography has become an accepted commodity. It is the enemy's trap for the minds of men.

Surely our sons need to learn what it means to love. No son is ready for marriage who has not learned to put others first—to forfeit his own desires for the sake of another person. Love, by its very nature, is an act of giving. Men who marry with a primary purpose of fulfilling their own needs and lust will be lousy husbands. Our sons need to know that their maturity is marked by their ability to put others first. That also means that they understand what the norm should be in a home where love prevails. Nothing can substitute for a home where the children regularly see their mother and father treating each other with respect and dignity, where the father puts the needs of his wife as a regular priority. When children are born, they enter an 18-20 year class called "How to treat a Husband or Wife." What we teach them, they learn! That is because we were created to be imitators. We learn from example. That does not mean that a child raised in a family of turmoil is destined to failure. God's grace is bigger than that. But we should not presume on God's grace. Nothing can prepare sons for marriage more effectively than being shown, year after year, how a godly husband treats his wife. There really is no substitute for that.

Likewise, the relationship between a son and his mother is an all important relationship. Here he finds his first introduction to the male/

female relationship. He comes to experience the tenderness of feminine nurturing, and to learn to relate to a woman. As he grows older, his relationship with his mother prepares him to understand how a woman thinks, how she views life, and how she reacts to situations. It is in this relationship that he begins to define himself as a man.

Preparing Daughters

Sons are trained to *leave;* daughters are trained to *be given.* As we have noted, the checks and balances in the whole courtship/betrothal scenario is grounded in the fact that the father is guardian over his daughter, so that any young man who is interested in her, will necessarily need to convince her father about his own intentions and abilities to became her guardian. That means that from the earliest age, parents must work to gain the trust of their daughter. A daughter who does not trust her father will never be willing to remain under his guardianship. When a suitor comes to her father, the father will have to make the decision whether such a relationship would be good for his daughter. Obviously, as a godly husband, he will seek the input of his wife and of his daughter in making such a decision. And if the daughter is clearly not interested in the young man, then there is no reason to pursue the matter. But if the daughter has come to trust her father, she will be able to abide by his decision when he says "no," even if the daughter thinks differently. Thus, the daughter must learn the beauty of submission to someone who loves her, and has proven he can be trusted. Once again, the most effective way for her to learn this is to observe her mother as she submits to her husband. A wife that regularly tries to manipulate her husband, or who disregards his role as head of the home, is preparing her daughter to rebel against his guardianship of her when the tough decisions need to be made.

Paul gives an interesting command to fathers (Col 3:21): "Fathers, do not exasperate your children, so that they will not lose heart." The word translated "exasperate" is ἐρεθίζω, *erethizo,* which means to provoke someone, and in this case, to provoke in a negative way. Fathers who regularly explode in anger, or who are overbearing, will fail to gain the trust of their daughters. They "lose heart," meaning that they give up hoping that there would ever be peace and protection in the home. Their thoughts move, instead, to the time they will be able to leave home. In such a scenario, a daughter would hardly be willing to trust her father to make the decision about her relationship with a young man, especially when that decision is viewed by her as the very means by which she could escape her father's provocations.

Perhaps the core issue here is that of selfishness. A father who is selfish in small things cannot be trusted to be open and giving in the large things. When a father constantly demonstrates that he is willing to give up his own interests in favor of what is good for his daughter, she will foster a trust in him that will stand her in good stead for the most important decisions of her life. Actually, in such a scenario, the daughter is relieved of all of the stress that comes upon young women in the current "dating scene." Measuring up to the expectations of the next "date" becomes an overwhelming stress for a young lady. If, when she arrives at the age of marriage, she has been fully convinced that her father has her best interests in mind, she will be far more comfortable allowing him to guard her in the important decision of marriage.

One of the primary ways that parents prepare their daughters for courtship is to teach them what modesty is, and the reason they should dress modestly. The reason God wants women to dress modestly is because they have the ability to be seductive. That is because men are attracted to what they see. Now just because a man is drawn to the *beauty* of a woman does not mean that she is being *seductive.* But the way she is dressed will have a profound influence on what kind of men are drawn to her. When a gal walks by, and a young man does an about-face, and hurries to catch up with her, he's not attracted to her intellect, or to the sweetness or gentleness of her spirit. He is attracted to her physical appearance. That is the way God created us. But if a woman dresses seductively, she will draw to herself men who have lust on their minds, because they sense she is willing to give them what they are seeking.

It is the father's responsibility to see that his daughter is dressed modestly, because it is his responsibility to guard her purity. But it is not the fault of a modestly dressed young lady if some young man has improper thoughts about her—that's his problem. The Bible does not require pretty girls to wear paper bags over their heads! That's something Mohammed thought up. So modesty is not the opposite of beautiful. In fact, as we noted earlier, one of the attributes of a virtuous woman is that she is beautiful in appearance as well as in her soul. Modesty is the opposite of being seductive. Modesty portrays genuine beauty; seductive dress encourages the lustful gazes (and actions) of men.

In general, modest dress means covering up. Plunging necklines, tight clothes, short skirts, bare midriff, etc. are not merely the current day fashion—they are the ways of the world that worships sex as a god. In reality, when a young lady leaves home dressed seductively, one should not first ask what is wrong with her. One should ask "why would her father let her out wearing that?"

The fact is, that many young ladies honestly do not understand how what they wear affects the thoughts of young men. And often, in believing homes, fathers are hesitant to speak openly to their wives and daughters about this issue, because if they do, they fear they might be accused of having a "dirty mind," or stooping to the perverse thoughts of the men of this world. But the reality is that men are attracted to what they see. How else could Yeshua have taught that a man could lust after a woman in his mind (Matt 5:28): "but I say to you that everyone who looks at a woman with lust for her has already committed adultery with her in his heart." I dare say that if godly women actually knew what men think, it would change the way they select their clothing.

It is true that men are required to keep their thoughts pure, and not to allow what they see to pull them further into lustful thoughts and emotions. And it is further true that a man who lusts is responsible for his own sin. But why would godly women want to make the men in their community stare at the ceiling while talking together? Wives dressed modestly honor the Lord and their husbands, and daughters dressed modestly honor the Lord and their fathers.

So there is a very good reason why a father is responsible to guard the modesty of his daughter: he knows how a man thinks, and what a man sees. And he remembers what it was like as a young man anticipating a relationship with a young lady. A daughter who learns to trust her father will also trust his judgment when it comes to whether something is modest or not.

But we should get one matter straight: dressing modestly does not overcome sexuality, nor should it. Unfortunately, in the emerging Christian Church, the neo-platonism that characterized her theology forever put sexuality as a "dirty word," connected with the material aspects of this creation, as over against the non-physical world of "spiritual piety." As a result, we can hardly talk about matters of sexuality without thinking that we have entered into a forbidden realm. But let's not kid ourselves: the courting relationship is a sexual relationship, and it should be. It is not a sexual relationship of consummation, but it is sexual, nonetheless. If a young man comes saying he wants permission to talk with your daughter about next Shabbat's *parashah,* you know he's not telling the whole story! He's attracted to your daughter because she is feminine, and beautiful, and that's the way God intended it. It is the father's obligation to guard the morality of his daughter, by carefully selecting the kind of man that he feels is suitable for her, and by monitoring their growing friendship to make sure that wisdom prevails—that they are not put into compromising situations in which they might give way to their own weaknesses.

So dressing modestly does not have its purpose in covering up beauty. It simply has its purpose in covering up.

Obviously, the father-daughter relationship is the primary preparation for courtship. As the daughter is trained to respect her father, she is learning what it will be like to respect her future husband. Moreover, her relationship with her father is training her how to build a relationship with a man—the way a man thinks, looks at the world, talks, or doesn't talk, and the different ways that a man responds to various situations. The first male lap she sits on is her father's; the first kisses and hugs she gets from a man are from her dad. It is important, then, for fathers to have a healthy, fatherly, physical relationship with their daughters. In so doing, they are giving them their first experience in the mysterious male/female relationship.

How utterly devastating when a father abuses a daughter! Physical abuse and molestation crushes a life and is often impossible to repair completely. Scars of child abuse remain for a life-time. By God's grace, many are returned to productive and joyful lives, but it is only after much trauma, many, many tears, and hard work in forgiveness.

Because, in our times, child molestation is so prevalent, some Godly fathers might shy away from showing physical affection to their daughters. This would be a great sorrow. Family affection is an important ingredient in training our children for the relationship of marriage. Men who are not as open about showing physical affection should work hard to overcome their hesitancy and express their love in tangible and physical ways.

In terms of specifics, a daughter needs to be trained how the courtship procedures work, and how they don't. First, a young girl needs to be given training how to deal with a young man who may approach her. In our day, most young men haven't ever heard of courtship, so they're clueless about what is right and what is not. There's no need to be rude, but a young girl needs to know how to say "no." A guy that constantly "hangs around" may not do anything out of order, but if the young girl is uncomfortable with his presence, she needs to be able to express her discomfort in appropriate ways.

In situations that may occur outside of the community, where young men she does not know may approach her, she needs to be prepared to let them know she is not interested in their approaches. In this case, she should know that if her first rebuffs are not heeded, being "rude" is okay. In our society, where many young men have no scruples, she needs to know how to be blunt, and she needs to know that being blunt in these kinds of situations is okay.

A young woman also needs to know how to respond to a man who approaches her honorably and with respect. There is no need for rebuff here, but she needs to be ready to say, "You'll need to talk with my father." Since we're only now trying to recover a biblical mode of courtship, we will need to teach our daughters to respond in this way. As she responds by showing the respect she has for her father's authority, she will likewise be telling the young man that he too must have a similar respect.

If, and when, a young man does approach her father, this does not necessarily mean anything will come of it. Obviously, the father will make his own assessment first. If he thinks the young man is not suitable, that's where it will end, at least for the present. If the parents think there is a possible match, the matter will be taken up with their daughter. If she's not interested, that will be the end of it, at least for the present. In such a scenario, however, if the parents think it is something that might be pursued, they should commit themselves to prayer, and even suggest that their daughter do the same. If the relationship is something God intends to be nurtured, then He will have to change the young girl's perspective. Obviously, if her perspective does not change, the relationship could never be fostered.

Here, again, the primary responsibility is laid upon the shoulders of the father as the guardian of his daughter. He protects her purity as well as her feelings and her emotions. He safeguards her until such time as he is able to transfer his guardianship to the man that has proven himself, both to the parents as well as to the young lady, that he is capable and willing to take on the responsibilities of a husband.

Thus, the subject of courtship should be something regularly spoken of as a daughter grows up. Talking together about her dreams and desires, her likes and dislikes, as well as God's plan for marriage, all become the important training sessions as a daughter is prepared for courtship.

Courtship in our Modern World

It is one thing to talk about the *idea* of courtship and betrothal, and quite another thing to actually implement it in our modern world. It seems far more possible in secluded communities than it would for families living within the mix of our modern society. By "secluded communities" I'm referring to groups like the Amish or Mennonites, or the ultra-orthodox Jewish communities that primarily fence themselves off from the surrounding society. Their young people are far less influenced by the expectations and pressures our upside-down world exerts upon our children. But even they are not entirely immune.

Like it or not, the television, movies, advertisements, magazines, novels, music, and commercialism in our world all shout a unified message: a young girl is "weird" if she doesn't have a boyfriend, and there's something wrong with a young man who isn't paired off with a girlfriend. Raising our children to have a biblical perspective about male/female relationships is therefore a formidable challenge.

What is more, the general perspective of the Christian Church on this matter is really no different than that of the world. Youth groups and social activities within the Church are very often built upon the societal norm that young guys and gals should naturally begin to "find each other" in their early teens. Most parents can't think outside of this box either. This means that as our children make friends with families from main-line Christian churches, they will be influenced by this same mentality. It doesn't mean that they will inevitably accept it, but they will be influenced by it.

The key to overcoming the pressures of our society that call our children to engage in emotional male/female relationships lies in the hands of parents, and particularly the father. Since the Scriptures provide the pattern of a father guarding the purity of his daughter, it is on his shoulders as guardian that the success of courtship depends. That means, of course, that as children grow and mature, they must be continually taught about the beauty and sanctity of marriage, and that a young man's approach to a young lady must always involve her father.

But we must also overcome the mentality, so prevalent in our times, that having an exclusive friendship with someone of the opposite sex is a necessary "training ground" for eventually being married. Young people need to realize that courtship begins a serious relationship that hopefully will culminate in marriage. In other words, courtship is not simply supervised dating. The idea that a young man and woman will simply "get to know each other as friends" without any notion of possible marriage is outside the scope of courtship. That means that if a young man is interested in one's daughter, the first thing to ascertain is whether he is an acceptable candidate to become her husband. If he is not, there's no good reason to encourage an exclusive friendship between the two of them. In fact, there are a lot of reasons why such an exclusive friendship should not be encouraged. From the young man's viewpoint, he should not be approaching a young lady with his interests
in her unless he has already decided that she is someone he would like to marry.

So the procedure is really pretty straightforward:

1. A young man lets a young woman know of his interests, either directly to her, or to her father. If he approaches the young lady in an appropriate way, her immediate response should be "you'll need to talk with my father." If he continues to approach her without talking to her father, the father should take the initiative to let him know the proper protocol. His willingness to comply is the first indication that he is honorable.

2. Once the young man has spoken with the girl's father, he should let the young man know that he'll get back to him in a few days. Of course, the father should be courteous and gracious: the whole matter of a young man approaching a girl's father is itself a bit traumatic.

3. The father, together with his wife, should ascertain if they think the suitor is an acceptable candidate for their daughter's hand. If they have significant issues with the young man, he should be contacted, and graciously and kindly told that his desire to court the young lady is not acceptable. It would also be wise to speak with the young man's parents, to assure them that while the whole procedure has been honorable, the "match" just doesn't seem right.

    If, however, the daughter's parents are favorable toward the

suitor's request and the daughter herself agrees, then he should be
invited to begin to spend time with the family. This gives younger
siblings a real life example of how the courting procedure works.
Once again, there should be open and regular communication with
the young man's parents.

4. As the courting continues, if there comes a time when the girl's
    parents or the daughter sense it is not a good match, then it is the
    father's duty to explain to the young man that he is no longer free
    to develop an exclusive friendship with his daughter. The father
    will need to be extremely gracious yet equally firm. No doubt,
    such a decision will hopefully be affirmed by the young girl as
    well. The best way to avoid this difficult situation is to make wise
    judgements about the suitor from the very beginning. Moreover,
    as soon as the girl's parents conclude that the young man is not for
    their daughter, they should put an end to the courting immediately
    and not allow it to drag out. Nothing is gained by postponing the
    difficult discussion with the young man.

5. As the courting continues, the young lady will no doubt spend time
    with the suitor's family as well, provided that his family has the
    same perspective, and that their time together will always be super-
    vised. At no time should the couple carry on their courtship unsu-
    pervised. If the young man is not living with his family, courtship
    activities should be done with the young lady's family, or in public
    surroundings where the couple remains accountable.

6. As the relationship progresses, the young man should ask the girl's
    father for her hand in marriage. The length of the courtship will
    depend on many factors, but once again, this is primarily in the
    hands of the girl's father. If the suitor asks for her hand in mar-
    riage, and the father is not certain they are ready, he can simply say
    that it is not yet the right time, and encourage them to continue in
    their courtship. On the other hand, a suitor with "cold feet" may
    need some urging. If the girl's parents sense that the time is right
    for them to marry, and the girl agrees, the girl's father should talk
    to the young man and encourage him to take the step of betrothal.

7. Once a formal betrothal has been arranged, it is wise to set the
    specific date for the wedding. Too much time between the betrothal
    and the wedding is not wise, but there should be sufficient time to
    plan and prepare for the wedding without causing undue stress and

financial burden. Traditionally betrothal was for a year. But there is no reason why the betrothal could not be shorter than this, especially if the courtship has been given sufficient time.

Singles Living on Their Own

In the ancient world, a young lady would remain with her family until she was married, regardless of her age. As noted before, this provided her with the protection and guardianship she needed, either by her father or other male family members. In our world, however, there are significant numbers of young adult ladies living on their own. In any Torah community, single ladies living on their own will inevitably be part of the congregation. What should be the procedure for these single ladies when approached by a suitor?

It would seem wise for the single lady to seek out a married couple in the community who would act as her guardian. In this case, the husband and wife together would provide the single lady the guardianship and counsel she needs in the courting process. Once such a relationship has been established, men who may approach the single lady regarding a desire for exclusive friendship should be directed to the married couple, in the same way that a daughter would send a would-be suitor to her father. The courtship would then proceed as outlined above. Of course, this is presuming that the girl's parents are either geographically distant, or for some other reason unable or unwilling to act on her behalf. There should be care given that the courting couple not spend unsupervised time alone. Their time together should either be at the married couple's home, or in a public setting where there is clear accountability.

What about the situation where a single lady living on her own shows interest in a single man? In this case, the man should encourage her to find a married couple in the community who would act as her guardian. Her willingness to comply would be a strong indicator of her ability to submit to authority, and her willingness to follow the biblical pattern in which a woman is "given" in marriage. Where neither the single lady or man are interested in following a courtship model, it will become the duty of the elders/overseers in the community to approach them, and explain the concepts of courtship and betrothal. Here again, the elders/overseers could suggest to the single lady that she select an appropriate married couple to act in the place of her father.

In our times, there are a growing number of families without resident fathers. In such cases, the mother will need to act in the place of the father, and provide the covering for her daughter in courtship matters. Here again, it would be wise for this single mother to seek out the counsel and advice of a married couple in the community as she guides her daughter through courtship to betrothal and marriage. This is because the perspectives and insight of a man is an important part in the guardianship of a daughter.

What about a situation where a believing wife is married to an unbelieving husband? The first task will be for the wife to convince her husband that the courtship model is good, and that it will provide the best protection for their daughter. If he is willing to take the responsibility of guarding her during the courtship process, then he should be encouraged to do just that. Perhaps the realization of his duty in this matter might be used of the Lord to open his eyes to his own spiritual needs. If, on the other hand, the unbelieving husband wants no part of the courtship procedure, the wife should seek his agreement that she be allowed to function as the daughter's protection and guardian. In such a case, she would be wise to seek the counsel of a married couple within the community as she guides her daughter through courtship and betrothal. Yet even if the unbelieving husband does not want to fulfill his role in this matter, he should not be disregarded. The wife should regularly seek his advice and input for decisions that will be made for the daughter.

In the case where a woman's husband has died, and she is seeking to be remarried, as noted above, Paul states that she is "free to be married to whom she wishes, only in the Lord" (1Cor 7:39). Even though she is not required to "be given" in this case, and thus does not need a guardian, it would still be wise for her to seek out the counsel of a married couple to guide her through the courtship and betrothal process.

The issue of remarriage after a divorce is fraught with many difficulties, yet it is something that will inevitably be faced in our times, since divorce has become so prevalent in our society. It is impossible to set down guidelines that will fit each case of a divorcee seeking to remarry. Each case will need to be handled with regard to its own unique issues and difficulties. Regardless, it is the better part of wisdom for a divorced woman, who is seeking remarriage, to find a married couple to give her counsel and to provide guardianship and accountability.

In each of the above scenarios, where a married couple is sought for their guardianship and counsel, it is important that the couple act together. It is extremely unwise for a husband to act alone in providing guardianship and counsel for a single woman. To do so is usually a formula for disaster.

Courtship with Someone Outside of the Community

The above scenarios presume that those involved in the courtship and betrothal process are all within the same community, meaning that they have, to one degree or another, the same perspective on matters of faith and *halachah*. An entirely different scenario presents itself when a young man or woman becomes interested in someone outside of the community. The best result in such a case would be if the family of the young man or woman would join the community, but this is usually not what happens. In the case where a young man outside of the community shows interest in a young lady within the community, the young lady's father becomes the controlling factor. His guardianship over his daughter provides the necessary guidelines for the courtship. Her parents will need to make the important decision regarding whether the suitor's faith and practice are substantially in concert with those of their daughter. His attendance at the community meetings should not be considered a substantial guarantee of either his faith or his manner of life. Too often a young man who is interested in a young lady will do whatever is needed during courtship days to win her hand.

Even more difficult is the case where a young man is interested in a young lady who is outside of the community. In this case, one cannot presume that her father is even aware of his biblical responsibility to act as her guardian, or that he would seriously apply himself to such a role even if he were aware of it. The girl's home, then, may not be a suitable place in which courtship can take place. Even upstanding Christian homes will often have accepted the world's standards when it comes to issues of dating. Courtship will be a foreign concept. Given such a scenario, the courtship should take place in the home of the young man as much as possible. Moreover, the young lady should be taught the ways of Torah and encouraged to join the community as much as possible.

It can be readily seen that in these situations, the deepest problem is that, apart from the families of the young man or woman joining the community, courtship with someone outside of the community separates that person from his or her family and their community of faith. And even more, in the case where a young lady is interested in a man who is outside of the community, given the eventuality of marriage, she will be obligated to leave her family and join with her husband, thus leaving the Torah community. Inevitably, courtship with those who are outside of the community will often result in the inability to pass a Torah way of life to the next generation.

Still, given the fact that Torah communities are few, and are often small in numbers, it seems likewise inevitable that some of our children will marry believers outside of the community. We can only hope and pray that those they do marry will be persuaded of the value of Torah life and remain within the Torah community. Surely the period of courtship will be the best place to teach and live out the ways of Torah before the young man or woman who comes in from another faith community, with the hope that a hunger for God's ways will be nurtured within them and that they will therefore desire to join the Torah community. In the end, it will be the spiritual strength and determination of our own children that will be the deciding factor.

Patience and Perseverance

Obviously, what I have suggested here regarding courtship and betrothal is the ideal. Any Torah community in our times will be charting new waters in this whole matter. This means that there must be patience and forbearance, as well as perseverance. Some families will be hesitant to embrace this way of thinking, since it runs so cross-grain to our society's standards and norms. They will fear that they run the risk of leaving their children "out of the loop," never to marry. So to put this biblical pattern of marriage into practice, it will require a growing faith on the part of parents, and a perseverance in prayer, that God will bring the right husband or wife for their children.

Yet it is clear that if we expect to pass on a Torah kind of faith to the next generation, this matter of courtship and betrothal is pivotal. We cannot expect the next generation to live in obedience to God's commandments if they marry those who have been taught that the Torah has been abolished. Ultimately, as in all things, we are left up to God's mercies. We may trust Him for the future of our children, and thus for the manner in which our children will take this message of truth into the next generation.

All He requires of us is that we remain faithful. He will do the rest.

Let's Talk About It

1. How is courting a better alternative to dating?

2. What is the difference between dating and courting?

3. What is a father's roll in the courting scenario? Discuss the role of single mothers in the courting procedures.

4. How should we approach courting for older singles?

5. What should we do if our children desire to enter into courtship outside of the community?

Chapter 8
Marriage in a Fallen World: Divorce

After spending a good deal of time focusing our attention on the blessings of marriage, and how we can prepare ourselves and our children for this blessing, it may seem like a "left turn" to venture into the dark waters of divorce. After all, why should we discuss failed marriages when we have every right to expect that our marriages will succeed? Since we believe that God blesses those who walk in His ways, then we should expect that as we implement His view of marriage and discipline ourselves to obey His Torah through the strength He provides, we should focus on the positive outcomes rather than the negative. Or so it would seem.

But studying what the Scriptures have to say about divorce will be good for us in a number of ways. First, it will help us to avoid divorce. Divorce is a reality in our world—that is a given. Since people are sinners, our sinful choices bring consequences. This is just as true in the realm of marriage as it is in all other realms. In some ways, marriage is like a delicate yet beautiful glass sculpture. It's beauty exists, in measure, because of its fragility. We must be aware, then, that sinful choices of a husband and wife may easily break the exquisite beauty of the marriage relationship. It is not that we go about in fear that our marriages may crumble. Rather, we understand that any relationship, and particularly a relationship as deep as marriage, is something that must be guarded and nurtured. When a husband or wife fails to guard the precious gift of their relationship, they become vulnerable to the demise of sin, and their marriage is at risk.

Secondly, the body of Messiah is made up of people, many of whom came to salvation after a life of unbelief. Before coming to seek God's forgiveness and grace, they may have accepted the world's viewpoint of things, and may have experienced marriages that ended in divorce. They have been forgiven, and have been made new. Yet the scars of their broken relationships may still have some affect upon their perspective and current relationships. It is therefore important that they gain God's perspective about divorce, and give themselves, in their current relationships, to God's way of doing things.

Thirdly, the primary victims of divorce are the children. Chil-

dren are deeply affected by the divorce of their parents. Owing to no fault
of their own, children who come from broken families may carry into
their own marriages a warped view of how conflicts in marriage are to be
handled. They may have the mistaken viewpoint that, as painful as divorce
is, it is still a viable option when differences between themselves and their
spouse may seem irreconcilable. Moreover, as the number of divorces
continues to rise in our times, it is inevitable that divorced singles within
any given congregation will also increase. This often brings the question
of whether a divorced person can remarry to the forefront. Understanding
what the Scriptures teach about divorce is therefore essential in making
Godly decisions about remarriage.

Finally, studying what the Bible says about divorce will aid us in
ministering to those who have been divorced, or who are contemplating
divorce. All too often the ways of the world are considered the norm when
the issues of divorce arise. We must retool our thinking along biblical lines
in order to offer God's perspective and teaching to those who find themselves in a marriage that is failing.

As we approach the whole matter of divorce, there are some important fundamentals that should be stated up-front. First is the fact that
divorce is not an unforgiveable sin. Sometimes people who have come to
faith in Messiah, but who have been divorced, are made to feel like they
are second-class citizens in the kingdom of God. This is wrong. All of us
are sinners saved by God's grace. Our sin was laid upon Yeshua, and He
bore the penalty for them. In creating us a new in Yeshua, old things have
passed; all things have become new.

Secondly, in spite of the fact that divorce has become an acceptable
alternative in our times, we must resolutely adhere to what the Scriptures
tell us about God's perspective about divorce: He hates it! (Mal 2:16)
God intends that marriage should last a life time. That is the only way that
marriage fulfills its purpose in portraying His own relationship with His
chosen people. While God allows divorce in certain situations, such allow-
ance should not overshadow the fact that divorce is not what He desires.
Divorce is allowed by God in some instances because in a fallen world,
things have been broken beyond repair. But divorce is always the result of
sin and unbelief. It is not something offered by God as a viable way out of
one's commitment.

Thirdly, as we have seen, marriage is revealed by God as a covenant, a covenant that is enacted by taking an oath. Wrongful divorce, then,

is a breach of one's oath. Breaking an oath is very serious and brings dire consequences.

All of these things mean that we must do our best to understand divorce from a biblical perspective, and not fall prey to thinking that divorce as defined by our modern world is acceptable in God's eyes.

Four Primary Texts

There are four primary texts in the Scriptures that deal with divorce: Deuteronomy 24:1–4; Matthew 5:32; Matthew 19:3–12; 1Corinthians 7:10–16. We will briefly study each of these as we seek to understand what the Scriptures teach us about divorce.

Deuteronomy 24:1–4

MT	Lxx	NASB
1 כִּי־יִקַּח אִישׁ אִשָּׁה וּבְעָלָהּ וְהָיָה אִם־לֹא תִמְצָא־חֵן בְּעֵינָיו כִּי־מָצָא בָהּ עֶרְוַת דָּבָר וְכָתַב לָהּ סֵפֶר כְּרִיתֻת וְנָתַן בְּיָדָהּ וְשִׁלְּחָהּ מִבֵּיתוֹ 2 וְיָצְאָה מִבֵּיתוֹ וְהָלְכָה וְהָיְתָה לְאִישׁ־אַחֵר 3 וּשְׂנֵאָהּ הָאִישׁ הָאַחֲרוֹן וְכָתַב לָהּ סֵפֶר כְּרִיתֻת וְנָתַן בְּיָדָהּ וְשִׁלְּחָהּ מִבֵּיתוֹ אוֹ כִי יָמוּת הָאִישׁ הָאַחֲרוֹן אֲשֶׁר־לְקָחָהּ לוֹ לְאִשָּׁה 4 לֹא־יוּכַל בַּעְלָהּ הָרִאשׁוֹן אֲשֶׁר־שִׁלְּחָהּ לָשׁוּב לְקַחְתָּהּ לִהְיוֹת לוֹ לְאִשָּׁה אַחֲרֵי אֲשֶׁר הֻטַּמָּאָה כִּי־תוֹעֵבָה הִוא לִפְנֵי יְהוָה וְלֹא תַחֲטִיא אֶת־הָאָרֶץ אֲשֶׁר יְהוָה אֱלֹהֶיךָ נֹתֵן לְךָ נַחֲלָה ס	1 ἐὰν δέ τις λάβη γυναῖκα καὶ συνοικήσῃ αὐτῇ καὶ ἔσται ἐὰν μὴ εὕρῃ χάριν ἐναντίον αὐτοῦ ὅτι εὗρεν ἐν αὐτῇ ἄσχημον πρᾶγμα καὶ γράψει αὐτῇ βιβλίον ἀποστασίου καὶ δώσει εἰς τὰς χεῖρας αὐτῆς καὶ ἐξαποστελεῖ αὐτὴν ἐκ τῆς οἰκίας αὐτοῦ 2 καὶ ἀπελθοῦσα γένηται ἀνδρὶ ἑτέρῳ 3 καὶ μισήσῃ αὐτὴν ὁ ἀνὴρ ὁ ἔσχατος καὶ γράψει αὐτῇ βιβλίον ἀποστασίου καὶ δώσει εἰς τὰς χεῖρας αὐτῆς καὶ ἐξαποστελεῖ αὐτὴν ἐκ τῆς οἰκίας αὐτοῦ ἢ ἀποθάνη ὁ ἀνὴρ ὁ ἔσχατος ὃς ἔλαβεν αὐτὴν ἑαυτῷ γυναῖκα 4 οὐ δυνήσεται ὁ ἀνὴρ ὁ πρότερος ὁ ἐξαποστείλας αὐτὴν ἐπαναστρέψας λαβεῖν αὐτὴν ἑαυτῷ γυναῖκα μετὰ τὸ μιανθῆναι αὐτὴν ὅτι βδέλυγμά ἐστιν ἐναντίον κυρίου τοῦ θεοῦ σου καὶ οὐ μιανεῖτε τὴν γῆν ἣν κύριος ὁ θεὸς ὑμῶν δίδωσιν ὑμῖν ἐν κλήρῳ	1 "When a man takes a wife and marries her, and it happens that she finds no favor in his eyes because he has found some indecency in her, and he writes her a certificate of divorce and puts it in her hand and sends her out from his house, 2 and she leaves his house and goes and becomes another man's wife, 3 and if the latter husband turns against her and writes her a certificate of divorce and puts it in her hand and sends her out of his house, or if the latter husband dies who took her to be his wife, 4 then her former husband who sent her away is not allowed to take her again to be his wife, since she has been defiled; for that is an abomination before the LORD, and you shall not bring sin on the land which the LORD your God gives you as an inheritance.

This is the text used by the scholars who approached Yeshua about the issue of divorce (Matt 19:7, cf. Matt 5:31). It is one of the primary texts of the Torah dealing with the issue of divorce.

The opening phrase emphasizes that a legitimate marriage is in view: "When a man takes a wife and marries her ...." The additional phrase "and marries her" (literally, "and he becomes her husband," cf. Deut 21:13) emphasizes the legitimate nature of the union. It happens that the husband turns against his wife ("she finds no favor in his eyes") because he has found some "indecency in her," בָהּ עֶרְוַת דָּבָר, *bah 'ervat davar.* Deciphering what is meant by *'ervat davar* has been troublesome for commentators and scholars. If the issue were one of sexual infidelity through an act of adultery, then the death penalty would be enacted (Lev 20:10). If he suspected her of adultery, but there was insufficient evidence to prove it, he would be required either to forego any further action in the matter, or require his wife to undergo the test of the bitter water (Num 5:11ff). We should presume, then, that *'ervat davar* describes something other than adultery or suspected adultery. The Hebrew word עֶרְוָה, *'ervah* often means "naked" (e.g., it is used regularly in describing sexual relations in Lev 18), and sometimes is used euphemistically for the genitals. It is also used metaphorically of unguarded regions of a land (e.g., Gen 42:9, 12). But the word also came to mean something indecent or inappropriate, as in the requirement that excrement not be in the camp, for such would be "indecent" (Deut 23:15).

The fact that the word often means "naked" was taken by some to indicate that in our text, the *'ervat davar,* the "indecent thing" referred to a wife who constantly dressed immodestly. Some would add to this the character of being a flirt. The Sages, in one place, seem to interpret the passage with the idea that a flirtatious wife has also cast her eyes upon another man, and that this has become evident to her husband. Apparently, the wife was unwilling to relent of her desire for the other man, and thus the divorce was permitted.

> It has been taught: R. Meir used to say: As men differ in their treatment of their food, so they differ in their treatment of their wives. Some men, if a fly falls into their cup, will put it aside and not drink it. This corresponds to the way of Papus b. Judah who used, when he went out, to lock his wife indoors. Another man, if a fly falls into his cup, will throw away the fly and then drink the cup. This corresponds to the way of most men who do not mind their wives talking with their brothers and relatives. Another man, again, if a fly falls into his soup, will squash it and eat it. This corresponds to the way of a bad man who sees his wife go out with her hair unfastened and spin cloth in the street with her arm pits uncovered and bathe with the men. Bathe with the men, you say? — It should be, bathe in the same place as the men. Such a one it is a religious duty to divorce, as it says, because he has found some unseemly thing in her . . . and he sends her out of his house and she goes and becomes another man's wife. The text calls him 'another', implying that he is not the fellow of the first; the one expelled a bad woman from his house, and the other took a bad woman into his house. If the second is fortunate, he will also send her away, as it says, and the latter husband hates her, and if not she will bury

him, as it says, or if the latter husband die; he deserves to die since the one expelled a wicked woman from his house and the other took her into his house. (b.*Gittin* 90b)

When Yeshua comments on this passage, however, He says:

Matt 19:7 They said to Him, "Why then did Moses command to give her a certificate of divorce and send her away?" 8 He said to them, "Because of your hardness of heart Moses permitted you to divorce your wives; but from the beginning it has not been this way. 9 "And I say to you, whoever divorces his wife, except for immorality, and marries another woman commits adultery."

Note the perspective of the scholars: "Moses commanded (ἐντέλλω) to give her a certificate of divorce," while Yeshua responds "Moses permitted (ἐπιτρέπω) you to divorce your wives." Here our Master gives us a keen insight into the Deuteronomy passage. Moses never commanded a man to divorce his wife—the passage simply describes what happened in the course of life in ancient Israel. Yeshua's point is that while the Torah dealt with the hardened heart of men, it never commanded divorce. In fact, the Deuteronomy passage is not directly dealing with the divorce itself, but with the issue of whether a divorced woman could return to her first husband after she had married another man. The answer, of course, is that she could not. In other words, the primary purpose of the Deuteronomy text is to prohibit men from treating a woman as property to be traded back and forth.

It may well have been that the wife in our text was innocent of her husband's suspicions. Yet because he had set his heart against her because he found in her some indecent matter, she was vulnerable for emotional abandonment or even abuse. Moreover, since ancient Israel had given in to polygamy, a wife who fell out of favor with her husband was vulnerable to the abuse of other wives who might have been in the home. Such a scenario would have made life a misery for her, and thus God permitted a divorce in order to free her from an unobservable situation.

As noted above, the primary emphasis of the Deuteronomy passage is that the woman who has been divorced, and married another man, is not permitted to her former husband. The three reasons given in the text are: 1) she has been defiled, 2) it is an abomination to the Lord, and 3) it causes the land to sin. These same three reasons, defilement, abomination, and pollution, are constantly repeated in connection with the sexual offenses of Lev 18 and 20. Thus, the primary purpose of the Deuteronomy passage is to maintain a holiness of sexual relations, it is not to give a legitimate cause for divorce.

Yeshua likewise teaches, in reference to Deuteronomy 24:1-4, that divorce was not God's will from the beginning. He returns to the foundational text of Gen 2:24, in which a husband and wife become one flesh, and thus are bound for life. From Yeshua's perspective, the only reason divorce is permitted in the Torah is because of the "hardness of heart." Here, the onus is put upon the husband. In finding some indecent matter in his wife, he has hardened his heart against her. She has no ability to change his heart, and as a result, she suffers. From Yeshua's perspective, the permission for divorce was to allow the woman freedom to be out from underneath a husband whose heart was hardened toward her. While the Sages interpreted Deut 24:1-4 as describing events that were the fault of the wife, Yeshua teaches that the fault was with the hardened heart of the husband.

Thus, while Deuteronomy 24 certainly describes the practice of divorce, its primary purpose is to deal with the issue of remarriage to a former husband after the woman has married a second time. *It is not primarily dealing with the definition of lawful divorce.* As such, the emphasis of this passage is the requirement for marriage to be taken seriously, and that a woman could not be treated as mere property to be traded back and forth between two men.

Matthew 5:31–32

Greek	NASB
31 Ἐρρέθη δέ· ὃς ἂν ἀπολύσῃ τὴν γυναῖκα αὐτοῦ, δότω αὐτῇ ἀποστάσιον. 32 ἐγὼ δὲ λέγω ὑμῖν ὅτι πᾶς ὁ ἀπολύων τὴν γυναῖκα αὐτοῦ παρεκτὸς λόγου πορνείας ποιεῖ αὐτὴν μοιχευθῆναι, καὶ ὃς ἐὰν ἀπολελυμένην γαμήσῃ, μοιχᾶται.	31 "It was said, 'Whoever sends his wife away, let him give her a certificate of divorce'; 32 but I say to you that everyone who divorces his wife, except for the reason of unchastity, makes her commit adultery; and whoever marries a divorced woman commits adultery.

In Yeshua's teaching here, typically called the "Sermon on the Mount," He is challenging the accepted interpretations of various Torah texts, offered by the teachers of the day. Here, as we noted above (in regard to Matt 19), He is at odds with the prevailing theology of some of the Sages regarding divorce, who considered that in some cases divorce was not only warranted, but required. Moreover, the school of Hillel had ruled that almost any matter could constitute grounds for legitimate divorce. The Mishnah records:

> The House of Shammai say, "A man should divorce his wife only because he has found grounds for it in unchastity, "since it is said, Because he has found in her indecency in anything (Dt. 24:1)." And the House of Hillel say, "Even if she spoiled his dish, "since it is said, Because he has found in her indecency in anything." R. Aqiba says, "Even if he found someone else prettier than she, "since it is said, And it shall be if she find no favor in his eyes (Dt. 24:1)." (m.*Gittin* 9:10)

By all the extant data, it appears that divorce was very prevalent in Yeshua's day. And, as this Mishnah notice tells us, it was because Deuteronomy 24 had been interpreted by Hillel (followed by the masses) in its widest possible sense.

Interestingly, Yeshua's interpretation follows that of the house of Shammai, who allowed divorce only in the case of unchastity (understanding עֶרְוַת דָּבָר of Deut 24 to be some kind of sexual sin). The Greek text uses πορνεία, *porneia,* which is translated "unchastity" in the NASB. *Porneia* (from which we have our English word "pornography") has a broad range of meanings. Generally, the word means "fornication," or any illicit sexual activity. It thus can encompass adultery, as well as all prohibited sexual relations, such as homosexuality, marriage too close to the bloodline (consanguinity), nudity, and prostitution.

The structure of the initial sentence that contains Yeshua's teaching is important. The basic sentence is: "everyone who divorces his wife makes her commit adultery." The exception clause, "except for the reason of unchastity," thus turns the sentence to the opposite, and could be construed thus: "everyone who divorces his wife for the reason of unchastity *does not* make her commit adultery." Thus, Yeshua clearly allows one legitimate reason for divorce: sexual infidelity.

We should also understand in regard to this passage that divorce is denoted in the biblical text by the term "send away" (ἀπολύω, *apoluo;* in the Hebrew, שָׁלַח, *shalach;* see BDAG, "ἀπολύω"), based upon the language of Deut 24. This does not denote "separation" as we know it in our times, where a spouse separates but is not divorced. Thus, Joseph first had it in his mind to dissolve his betrothal to Mary, which is also cast in the language of divorce: "And Joseph her husband, being a righteous man and not wanting to disgrace her, planned to send her away secretly" (Matt 1:19). In the current text (Matt 5:31-32), the NASB uses "send away" when quoting Deut 24:1, but translates the same word (*apoluo*) as "divorces" in v. 32. This is not inaccurate, for "to send away" does mean "to divorce."

Yeshua, therefore, gives one lawful cause for divorce: sexual infidelity. In such a case, the spouse who divorces for just causes is free to remarry without incurring transgression. However, a divorce, even though granted by the courts of men, but which is not sanctioned by God, is an unlawful divorce, and does not render either spouse free to remarry, since in God's eyes, they are still husband and wife. Therefore, Yeshua teaches that anyone who unlawfully divorces his wife "makes her commit adultery" (ποιεῖ αὐτὴν μοιξευθῆναι). This is because more often than not, a woman will need to remarry in order to maintain her living. This was especially the case in the ancient world, where the ability of a single woman to maintain a livelihood was almost non-existent. It is likely that rampant, unlawful divorce in the history of Israel was a root cause of prostitution. Moreover, Yeshua teaches that any man who marries a woman unlawfully divorced, commits adultery with her, since, in God's eyes, she is still the lawful wife of her husband. Thus, Yeshua's position on divorce and remarriage is based upon the sanctity of marriage. God considers marriage to be a life-long covenant, and He therefore severely limits the parameters of divorce in order to maintain its sanctity.

The parallel to our text in Luke emphasizes this aspect of Yeshua's words, for it leaves out the exception clause: "Everyone who divorces his wife and marries another commits adultery, and he who marries one who is divorced from a husband commits adultery" (Lk 16:18). Luke therefore intends his readers to focus upon the utter sanctity of marriage, and for this reason he leaves off the exception clause.

Matthew 19:3–12

The teaching of Yeshua on the matter of divorce and remarriage is also found in Matthew 19, parallel to Mark 10:1–12. Here, the Pharisees come to Yeshua, seeking not to know whether He agreed with Moses in Deut 24 regarding divorce, but what exactly His understanding was of the *'ervat davar* ("matter of unchastity") in the Torah text. More precisely, as we have seen, the issue related to the debates of the house of Hillel and the house of Shammai. Matthew's text helps us understand this by adding the words "for any cause" (which Mark does not have).

Greek	NASB
3 Καὶ προσῆλθον αὐτῷ Φαρισαῖοι πειράζοντες αὐτὸν καὶ λέγοντες· εἰ ἔξεστιν ἀνθρώπῳ ἀπολῦσαι τὴν γυναῖκα αὐτοῦ κατὰ πᾶσαν αἰτίαν; 4 ὁ δὲ ἀποκριθεὶς εἶπεν· οὐκ ἀνέγνωτε ὅτι ὁ κτίσας ἀπ᾽ ἀρχῆς ἄρσεν καὶ θῆλυ ἐποίησεν αὐτούς; 5 καὶ εἶπεν· ἕνεκα τούτου καταλείψει ἄνθρωπος τὸν πατέρα καὶ τὴν μητέρα καὶ κολληθήσεται τῇ γυναικὶ αὐτοῦ, καὶ ἔσονται οἱ δύο εἰς σάρκα μίαν. 6 ὥστε οὐκέτι εἰσὶν δύο ἀλλὰ σὰρξ μία. ὃ οὖν ὁ θεὸς συνέζευξεν ἄνθρωπος μὴ χωριζέτω. 7 λέγουσιν αὐτῷ· τί οὖν Μωϋσῆς ἐνετείλατο δοῦναι βιβλίον ἀποστασίου καὶ ἀπολῦσαι [αὐτήν]; 8 λέγει αὐτοῖς ὅτι Μωϋσῆς πρὸς τὴν σκληροκαρδίαν ὑμῶν ἐπέτρεψεν ὑμῖν ἀπολῦσαι τὰς γυναῖκας ὑμῶν, ἀπ᾽ ἀρχῆς δὲ οὐ γέγονεν οὕτως. 9 λέγω δὲ ὑμῖν ὅτι ὃς ἂν ἀπολύσῃ τὴν γυναῖκα αὐτοῦ μὴ ἐπὶ πορνείᾳ καὶ γαμήσῃ ἄλλην μοιχᾶται. 10 Λέγουσιν αὐτῷ οἱ μαθηταὶ [αὐτοῦ]· εἰ οὕτως ἐστὶν ἡ αἰτία τοῦ ἀνθρώπου μετὰ τῆς γυναικός, οὐ συμφέρει γαμῆσαι. 11 ὁ δὲ εἶπεν αὐτοῖς· οὐ πάντες χωροῦσιν τὸν λόγον [τοῦτον] ἀλλ᾽ οἷς δέδοται. 12 εἰσὶν γὰρ εὐνοῦχοι οἵτινες ἐκ κοιλίας μητρὸς ἐγεννήθησαν οὕτως, καὶ εἰσὶν εὐνοῦχοι οἵτινες εὐνουχίσθησαν ὑπὸ τῶν ἀνθρώπων, καὶ εἰσὶν εὐνοῦχοι οἵτινες εὐνούχισαν ἑαυτοὺς διὰ τὴν βασιλείαν τῶν οὐρανῶν. ὁ δυνάμενος χωρεῖν χωρείτω.	3 Some Pharisees came to Him, testing Him and asking, "Is it lawful for a man to divorce his wife for any reason at all?" 4 And He answered and said, "Have you not read that He who created them from the beginning made them male and female, 5 and said, 'For this reason a man shall leave his father and mother and be joined to his wife, and the two shall become one flesh'? 6 "So they are no longer two, but one flesh. What therefore God has joined together, let no man separate." 7 They said to Him, "Why then did Moses command to give her a certificate of divorce and send [her] away?" 8 He said to them, "Because of the hardness of your heart Moses permitted you to divorce your wives; but from the beginning it has not been this way. 9 "And I say to you, whoever divorces his wife, except for immorality, and marries another woman commits adultery." 10 The [His] disciples said to Him, "If the relationship of the man with his wife is like this, it is better not to marry." 11 But He said to them, "Not all men can accept the [this] statement, but only those to whom it has been given. 12 "For there are eunuchs who were born that way from their mother's womb; and there are eunuchs who were made eunuchs by men; and there are also eunuchs who made themselves eunuchs for the sake of the kingdom of heaven. He who is able to accept this, let him accept it."

The query of the Pharisees, then, was to ascertain Yeshua's own teaching regarding what *'ervat davar* (matter of unchastity) meant in Deut 24:1. Or more simply: did Yeshua side with Hillel or Shammai on the interpretation of *'ervat davar*? Yeshua's first retort was that they were asking the wrong question when it came to the issue of divorce. Instead of asking about the parameters of divorce, they should have been asking about the purpose of marriage in the first place. When we ask the wrong questions, we inevitable derive wrong answers. And so Yeshua points back to Gen 2:24 as the *crux interpretum* (the foundational point for interpretation). The question that should have been asked was this: "How is it possible that when God causes a husband and wife to be one, anyone could think of trying to severe this oneness?"

The Pharisees understood Yeshua's point, and this prompted their next question. "If no one should ever severe what God has joined together, why then did Moses *command* to give her a *get* (divorce document) and send her away?" As we noted in Matt 5:31-32, this is a misunderstanding of Deut 24 on the part of the Pharisees. Moses nowhere *commands* a husband to divorce his wife, regardless of what transgression she may have committed. It is to this misinterpretation that Yeshua thus responds: "Because of the hardness of your heart Moses *permitted* you to divorce your wives." Thus, Yeshua teaches that divorce is a provision in the context of hearts already hardened to God's primary purpose of marriage, i.e., the oneness of husband and wife.

What is the fuller import of the "hardness of your hearts?" We may venture several explanations. First, it may be the hardness of heart that is *unwilling* to forgive. Forgiveness, as we shall see, is a gift of the Spirit, enabling the heart of a believer to do what he or she otherwise would be unable to do. Forgiveness, then, is a fruit of the Spirit. Those who are born from above, however, may still grieve the Holy Spirit, that is, may still sin against the promptings of the Holy Spirit, and fail to obey what He is leading the individual to do. In such a scenario, the ability to restore the oneness within a marriage is lost, and (focusing upon the plight of a woman who has been falsely suspected of adultery) thus, divorce allows the wife to be free to remarry rather than be abandoned to the harshness of making her own livelihood.

Secondly, hardness of heart may be the *inability* to forgive. Where a spouse is not a believer, the ability to forgive may be lacking, bringing about a situation where a marriage is irreparably damaged. In such a case, divorce is once again given by God as a means of starting over.

Thirdly, hardness of heart may suggest a situation where trust and fidelity have been damaged beyond repair. It is not as though the individual is incapable of forgiveness, or unwilling to forgive. Indeed, forgiveness may have been exercised. But forgiveness does not necessarily restore relationship. In the case where a marriage relationship has been so deeply severed by the sin of infidelity, it may be impossible to restore genuine trust—something that is essential for the oneness principle upon which marriage itself is founded. In this case, divorce allows the innocent party to be free of the contractual restraints of marriage, and to seek remarriage if he or she so desires. Moreover, in a situation where sexual deviancy has been pervasive within the marriage, divorce may be the only way to guard children from the influence of such immorality.

After drawing their attention to the essential truths about God's intention for marriage, Yeshua goes on to give His explicit teaching regarding their initial question, i.e., what His interpretation was of the "matter of unchastity" (*'ervat davar*) in Deut. 24:1. He says: "And I say to you, whoever divorces his wife, except for immorality, and marries another woman commits adultery" (v. 9). Here, Yeshua focuses primarily upon the one man who is divorcing his wife. And once again, Yeshua includes the exception clause ("except for immorality") as He did in Matt 5:31–32, which governs the entire statement. If a man divorces his wife and remarries, he commits adultery. This is because an unlawful divorce does not dissolve his covenant responsibilities to his wife—in God's eyes, he is still married. Relations with another woman, then would be considered adultery. In this statement, Yeshua makes an indirect ruling regarding polygamy. If polygamy were lawful, then for a man to marry a second wife would have not been considered adultery, yet Yeshua rules that it is. The exception clause (as in 5:31–32) reverses the ruling of adultery in the case of remarriage: if a man divorces his wife because she has acted immorally, his divorce is lawful, and thus he is free to marry another woman.

The reaction of Yeshua's disciples is interesting. They realize that He has not only sided with the house of Shammai, in restricting divorce to a matter of sexual immorality, but that in so doing, He has effectively nullified the vast majority of divorces which were sanctioned by the ruling Sages. For proving a matter of sexual immorality by having a minimum of two witnesses, would have been nearly impossible. Their response suggests that they had given into the typical way of thinking in their day: divorce was the necessary "back door" that made commitment to a woman in marriage a possibility!

Before we condemn the view of the disciples, however, we should

consider the possibility that as followers of Yeshua, they had placed themselves in a vulnerable position, at least in terms of the current ruling body
of the Sanhedrin. If Yeshua were to be condemned as a blasphemer, they
too could be equally condemned if they persisted in claiming Him as their
leader, and teaching His doctrines. As such, an unbelieving wife might
become a witness against a believing husband in a matter that was deemed
a capital offense. The inability to divorce her in such a situation seemed
entirely unworkable.

Still, they had given into a somewhat prevalent idea of their day,
that a life-long commitment to one woman was more burdensome than
no involvement at all, something seen among certain Essenes and Greek
and Roman philosophers (cf. Josephus, *War* 2.120; *Ant.* 18.21; Philo, *Vit.
Cont.*; Ecclus 25:16–26; Davies-Allison, *Matthew,* 3.19, n. 90).

Yeshua's answer is surprising, for instead of condemning the idea
of celibacy, He notes that there is a proper place for it, but only to those
to whom "this word" is given (v. 11). This accords with the teaching of
Paul, that celibacy is a gift given to some for work in the kingdom (1Cor
7:7ff). Yeshua uses the term "eunuch" in an extended meaning, as "one
who remains single" and not merely in its more technical sense of a male
attendant in a Queen's court. Such an extended meaning may parallel texts
such as Isaiah 56:3, "Let not the foreigner who has joined himself to the
LORD say, 'The LORD will surely separate me from His people.' Nor let
the eunuch say, 'Behold, I am a dry tree.'" Yeshua gives three categories
of those who remain celibate, two of which were physically extant in His
day, and one which is a metaphoric extension: 1) eunuch by birth: This
corresponds to the rabbinic סְרִיס חַמָּה, literally "eunuch of the sun,"
meaning a boy who was born (from the first day of seeing the sunlight)
with the inability to procreate (b.*Yeb.*79b–80a); 2) eunuch by man: This
corresponds to the rabbinic סְרִיס אָדָם, literally "eunuch of man," meaning a male who had been castrated or through some accident (or birth) had
been injured so as to make procreation an impossibility; 3) eunuchs for the
kingdom of heaven: these are not physically eunuchs, nor are they impo-
tent by nature. They are indeed unmarried, not because they cannot take
a wife but rather because they will not in view of the duties placed upon
them by the kingdom of heaven. "For these people, the good and valuable
thing that marriage undoubtedly is (cf. vv. 3–9) must be turned down, sur-
rendered or sacrificed in view of the demand made upon them by something greater" (Davies-Allison, *Matthew,* 3.23). It seems most probable

that Yeshua here gives an explanation for His own celibacy.

The parallel to Matthew 19:3-12 in Mark 10:1–12 should also be explored for at least one additional aspect which Matthew does not include. In Mark 10:11–12, the action of divorce is reciprocal, including either the husband or the wife:

Greek	NASB
11 καὶ λέγει αὐτοῖς· ὃς ἂν ἀπολύσῃ τὴν γυναῖκα αὐτοῦ καὶ γαμήσῃ ἄλλην μοιχᾶται ἐπ᾽ αὐτήν· 12 καὶ ἐὰν αὐτὴ ἀπολύσασα τὸν ἄνδρα αὐτῆς γαμήσῃ ἄλλον μοιχᾶται.	11 And He said to them, "Whoever divorces his wife and marries another woman commits adultery against her; 12 and if she herself divorces her husband and marries another man, she is committing adultery."

It is usually remarked by commentators that Mark follows the Roman law, against that of the Jews, in stating that Yeshua recognized the legal ability of the wife to divorce her husband. Appeal to a quote from Joseph is likewise frequent: "But some time afterward, when Salome happened to quarrel with Costobarus, she sent him a bill of divorce, and dissolved her marriage with him, though this was not according to the Jewish laws; for with us it is lawful for a husband to do so; but a wife, if she departs from her husband, cannot of herself be married to another, unless her former husband put her away" (*Ant.* 15:259). It is true that rabbinic law never allowed a wife to give a *get* or a bill of divorcement to her husband. But what is often overlooked is that a wife could appeal to the courts when she had a legal right to be divorced, i.e., to be free from her marriage obligations to her present husband. The seeds of this are found in the Torah itself. For instance, in Ex 21:7ff, a woman who is sold as a slave, and then purchased for the purpose of marriage, has certain rights granted her. Apparently, if she is denied these rights, she has the ability to appeal to the court for justice.

In rabbinic law, certain failures on the part of the husband could give the right of appeal to the court by his wife. These included his refusal of conjugal rights, his failure to provide for her physical needs, physical abuse, apostasy, fornication, restricting his wife from her legal rights, as well as other things (see David Amram, *Jewish Law of Divorce* [Philadelphia, 1896], pp. 63ff). In such an appeal, if the wife proved her case, the court was obliged to require the husband to grant her a divorce. In practical measures, then, the wife pursued and obtained a divorce from her husband. And it appears from the Markan text that Yeshua agreed that such a procedure was lawful.

We may also comment briefly upon the more modern-day notion that separation, without remarriage, is not covered by the texts we have studied thus far. That is, in each case, it is when one "marries another" that the judgment of "adultery" is charged. The thinking is, then, that one can separate with impunity as long as one does not remarry. But this idea neglects a fundamental aspect of divorce in the ancient world, and in the time of Yeshua. Marriage was considered a binding covenant between the husband and wife, a covenant that required certain actions and afforded certain rights. There is no indication that Yeshua considered marriage differently. In other words, He considered the binding of husband to wife in marriage as requiring an on-going relationship of service to each other in light of the marriage covenant. Separation, by its very nature, means that such mutual service is suspended, meaning the covenant obligations would not be fulfilled. Such separation is therefore only permissible in the most extreme cases (cf. 1Cor 7 below).

It is not precisely clear how Yeshua would have ruled in matters of physical abuse, abandonment, failure to provide, and the other situations that the Jewish court would have ruled sufficient for divorce. It is clear that He did not consider many of the grounds for divorce offered by the rabbinic courts to be valid. Yet there is no indication that He condoned indefinite separation as an alternative where one spouse had clearly profaned the marriage covenant. His teaching in Matt 19/Mark 10 is specifically directed toward an interpretation of the *'ervat davar* of Deut 24. Whether He would have extended rightful divorce to other things, such as physical abuse and abandonment is left open in that He never comments specifically upon these scenarios. That Paul, as we shall see, extends divorce to abandonment, may indicate that Yeshua's single exception ("except for fornication") in the texts we have studied was understood more broadly than it has often been expounded.

1Corinthians 7

In 1Cor 7, Paul addresses the issues of marriage and divorce. While a full exposition of this passage is beyond the scope of our current study, it will be important for us to look at several verses that bear significantly upon the issue of divorce and remarriage. In this text, Paul is dealing with the issue of believers married to unbelievers. Especially in times of severe persecution, where followers of Yeshua were being imprisoned and put to death for their faith, marriage to an unbeliever could present significantly more difficult scenarios. Not only was the life and welfare of the believing spouse threatened, but the welfare of the children in the family was also a concern. Issues of separation in view of the preservation of life must therefore be considered.

Greek	NASB
10 Τοῖς δὲ γεγαμηκόσιν παραγγέλλω, οὐκ ἐγὼ ἀλλὰ ὁ κύριος, γυναῖκα ἀπὸ ἀνδρὸς μὴ χωρισθῆναι, 11 ἐὰν δὲ καὶ χωρισθῇ μενέτω ἄγαμος ἢ τῷ ἀνδρὶ καταλλαγήτω καὶ ἄνδρα γυναῖκα μὴ ἀφιέναι. 12 Τοῖς δὲ λοιποῖς λέγω ἐγὼ οὐχ ὁ κύριος· εἴ τις ἀδελφὸς γυναῖκα ἔχει ἄπιστον καὶ αὕτη συνευδοκεῖ οἰκεῖν μετ᾽ αὐτοῦ, μὴ ἀφιέτω αὐτήν· 13 καὶ γυνὴ εἴ τις ἔχει ἄνδρα ἄπιστον καὶ οὗτος συνευδοκεῖ οἰκεῖν μετ᾽ αὐτῆς, μὴ ἀφιέτω τὸν ἄνδρα. 14 ἡγίασται γὰρ ὁ ἀνὴρ ὁ ἄπιστος ἐν τῇ γυναικὶ καὶ ἡγίασται ἡ γυνὴ ἡ ἄπιστος ἐν τῷ ἀδελφῷ· ἐπεὶ ἄρα τὰ τέκνα ὑμῶν ἀκάθαρτά ἐστιν, νῦν δὲ ἅγιά ἐστιν. 15 εἰ δὲ ὁ ἄπιστος χωρίζεται, χωριζέσθω· οὐ δεδούλωται ὁ ἀδελφὸς ἢ ἡ ἀδελφὴ ἐν τοῖς τοιούτοις· ἐν δὲ εἰρήνῃ κέκληκεν ὑμᾶς ὁ θεός.	10 But to the married I give instructions, not I, but the Lord, that the wife should not leave her husband 11 (but if she does leave, she must remain unmarried, or else be reconciled to her husband), and that the husband should not divorce his wife. 12 But to the rest I say, not the Lord, that if any brother has a wife who is an unbeliever, and she consents to live with him, he must not divorce her. 13 And a woman who has an unbelieving husband, and he consents to live with her, she must not send her husband away. 14 For the unbelieving husband is sanctified through his wife, and the unbelieving wife is sanctified through her believing husband; for otherwise your children are unclean, but now they are holy. 15 Yet if the unbelieving one leaves, let him leave; the brother or the sister is not under bondage in such cases, but God has called us to peace.

In this chapter, Paul mentions the "present distress" (v. 26) and that the "time has been shortened" (v. 29). These indicate that he is giving his instructions in view of what he considers impending persecution. That such is the case informs his instructions about whether a father should give his virgin daughter in marriage (vv. 25ff). If persecution was imminent, Paul felt it better that a young lady not marry if she could remain single, because if she were to be pregnant or caring for an infant when the persecution came, it would be extremely hard to bear.

We should therefore keep in mind that imminent persecution most likely informs other aspects of the Apostle's *halachic* statements as well.

In v. 10, Paul instructs a wife to remain with her husband, but that if she leaves, she must remain unmarried. This would indicate that she did not have a valid divorce, but that she left her husband for other reasons. It appears that in this case and the next (where a husband is not to divorce his wife), Paul is addressing believers (since in vv. 12ff, he appears to address those who are married to unbelievers), and thus he reinforces the general teaching of Yeshua, that legitimate divorce is limited and that the norm is there should be no divorce.

Verses 12ff are addressed "to the rest," which appears to mean those who have an unbelieving spouse. The definition of "unbelieving" should not be a matter of speculation—it is not talking about levels of maturity, or conformity to a certain list of *halachot*. It means someone who has never confessed Yeshua to be the Messiah, or even someone who has denied Him to be the Messiah. The fear of some in Corinth was apparently that since they were one in marriage with an unbeliever, they might themselves be viewed as "unholy" by God. Paul makes it clear that this is not the case. Like the touch of Yeshua, that healed the unclean rather than contracting uncleanness to Himself, so the believing spouse "sanctifies" the unbeliever. Remaining married to an unbeliever, then, has salvific ramifications. It is not as though the unbeliever is granted righteousness on the basis of the believer's faith, but that in the course of living together, the unbeliever will see the life of faith in his or her spouse, and this may be what is used by God to bring that person to faith. Likewise, the children are given the advantage of a living witness, as well as the teaching that a believing spouse would offer.

However, if an unbelieving spouse "leaves" (χωρίζω, *chorizo*), the remaining, believing spouse is no longer "under bondage" (δουλόω, *douloo*). The questions pertaining to this *halachah* of the Apostle is what is meant by "leaving" and "under bondage." The Greek word *chorizo*, "to leave, separate" is used in marriage contracts of the 1st Century to denote "divorce" (see *BDAG*, "χωριζω"). We should most likely understand it similarly here. Furthermore, the idea of being "bound" within the marriage contract is likewise set forth by Paul in Romans 7 (though he uses a different word there, δέω, *deo*). He writes in Rom 7:2, "For the married woman is bound by law to her husband while he is living; but if her husband dies, she is released from the law concerning the husband." This metaphor of "being bound" in terms of the marriage covenant seems most likely that to which Paul refers in our text. Thus, when he writes that "the brother or the sister is not under bondage in such cases" (v. 15), he is saying that the marriage covenant has been dissolved. Or to put it another way, when an unbeliever divorces his or her believing spouse, abandoning the marriage, the believing spouse is no longer restrained by the marriage covenant: he or she is free to remarry.

Before we leave this brief survey of texts bearing upon the issue of divorce and remarriage, we should address several scenarios that regularly confront us. For instance, what about a person who divorces for unlawful reasons, and remarries before he or she becomes a believer in Yeshua? Is this marriage valid and acceptable within the believing community? The answer is "yes," the marriage is valid and acceptable, not on the basis of overturning what constitutes valid divorce and remarriage, but on the basis that when a person comes to faith in Messiah, "old things have passed, and new things have come" (2Cor 5:17). The believer in Yeshua is a "new creation," and as such, by God's grace, is to be received as having a "clean start." Couples in such a situation should do all in their power to make their marriage a vivid example of Messiah's love for His bride. It does not mean that some of the consequences of their previous marital failures will be erased. But they must face these consequences as those who have been given a new understanding of what God desires, and who have been given the power of the Spirit to face the events of life from the perspective of faith.

How do we deal with the situation where a believer divorces un-lawfully and then remarries. Clearly the Scriptures we have studied count this as adultery, and it should not be called anything less. Where such a person is unwilling to seek and demonstrate true repentance, he or she is to be dealt with according to the *halalchah* of 1Cor 5:11–12, which re-quires that someone who claims to be a believer but refuses to turn from immorality, is to be dismissed from the community. Yet if such a person does see the error of his or her ways, and demonstrates genuine repen-tance, there is no need for dismissal. The sin of adultery, while egregious, is not beyond forgiveness. Still, caution must be exercised. Repentance is not demonstrated by words alone, but by actions. The principle that governs the need for dismissal is "a little leaven leavens the whole lump of dough" (1Cor 5:6). For the sake of the community, and especially the children within the community, genuine repentance must be demonstrated before someone who has acted in such an immoral way would be allowed to remain within the congregation.

Another situation that is common in our day is for couples to engage in pre-marital sexual relations. What should the community do when such a couple seeks to be married with the blessing of the community? First, as soon as such a situation is discovered, it should be dealt with. If the couple is not willing to call their actions sin, and seek repentance, there is no choice but to dismiss them from the community, with the on-going hope that they will come to repentance and seek to be restored. If the situation does not come to light until they ask to be married, the leaders will need to assess the situation and come to agreement as to how the marriage should take place. Surely if the couple does not agree that their pre-marital relations were sinful, and if they are not willing to seek repentance for their sin, for the community to sanction and bless their marriage will be of little value. Their presence in the community will most likely have on-going negative effects. If they are willing to admit their sin, and seek repentance, it may be wise to require them to prove their repentance by remaining chaste with each other for a period of time, during which they would be accountable to someone within the community. This would not only prove the genuine nature of their repentance, but also prove to each other that their commitment is based upon more than physical attraction. Where a pregnancy has occurred out of wedlock, the girl's father or the community leaders (where there is no father) will need to have wisdom as to whether marriage to the father of the child is advisable or not. Once again, a demonstration of genuine repentance is the key to overcoming the effects of sin. However the leadership of the community chooses to deal with such scenarios, the outcome should be that the truth of Heb. 13:4 is demonstrated: "Marriage is to be held in honor among all, and the marriage bed is to be undefiled; for fornicators and adulterers God will judge."

Let's Talk About It

1. Is divorce ever legitimate in God's eyes? If so, on what grounds?

2. How should we treat someone who wants to be part of our community but has divorced their spouse on non-biblical grounds? What if the divorce occurred before they were saved?

3. What should a person do who is experiencing abuse from their spouse?

4. Share practical ways that you have found to strengthen your marriage.

5. Discuss the effect of divorce upon the children in the family.

Chapter 9
Knowing How to Forgive, and Doing It

In the last chapter, we surveyed a number of biblical texts dealing with divorce and remarriage. In many ways it is painful to study this material, for the simple reason that it is only truly applicable when a failure, characterized by sin, has taken place. Studying about divorce is like studying to be a coroner—it's about death. Of course, no one on their wedding day has divorce on his or her mind. So how does it happen? How do the wonderful plans of marriage, full of hope and excitement, turn into a battle that ends in the death of a relationship?

We could spend a great deal of time trying to analyze how husbands and wives grow apart, and how the seeds of an eventual divorce are sown. But I think it is more profitable to spend some time discussing the positive things for growing a marriage. There are some fundamental issues that either make or break relationship, and we do well to concentrate on these. We might use a car for an illustration. There are many small things that can go wrong with a car: a blinker light might burn out, windshield wipers might need to be changed, or brakes might be squeaking. These might be annoying, but they hardly make the car inoperative. However, if you run the car without any oil, or without water in the radiator, it will be ruined in short order! What I want to concentrate on in this chapter is the "oil" that keeps a marriage running.

Utilizing the Gift of Forgiveness

Learning to forgive someone who has hurt or offended us is an essential ingredient of maintaining relationships, and guarding our hearts against bitterness. Bitterness is to the soul what metal shavings are to an engine. If they are allowed to remain, failure is inevitable. But one does not overcome the ill effects of bitterness simply by trying hard not to be bitter. Bitterness is the fruit of an unforgiving heart. Conversely, learning to exercise forgiveness is the sure antidote to bitterness.

In fact, coming to understand the terrible effect of bitterness upon the soul is one good motivation to learn forgiveness. Bitterness and hatred are companions—the one gives birth to the other. Understanding how detrimental bitterness and hatred is to one's own emotional and spiritual health is important. It is like a cancer that eats away at the soul. Solomon wrote: "Better is a dish of vegetables where love is than a fattened ox served with hatred" (Prov. 15:17). Where bitterness and hatred reside, even life's finest things cannot be enjoyed.

Moreover, bitterness and hatred inevitably give way to slander. One cannot harbor ill feelings against someone else without eventually sharing these with others. Bitterness eventually outgrows the capacity of the soul to contain it. "Hatred stirs up strife, but love covers all transgressions" (Prov. 10:12); "He who conceals hatred has lying lips, and he who spreads slander is a fool" (Prov. 10:18).

Furthermore, bitterness and hatred, when they eventually consume the soul, change the very makeup of a person. I have personally known people who, unwilling to deal with their deep-seated bitterness against someone who hurt them, have changed to the extent that they suffered from all kinds of maladies, and even suffered emotional and mental breakdowns. Unwillingness to deal with their bitterness, they ended upon spoiling the lives of others as well: "See to it that no one comes short of the grace of God; that no root of bitterness springing up causes trouble, and by it many be defiled" (Heb. 12:15).

One more thing about bitterness: if it is allowed to remain, it grows (often in almost imperceptible ways), until it rules one's life. In fact, bitterness is a gateway for the enemy of our souls to gain a foothold in our lives. Paul links the two in Eph 4:26-27, "Be angry, and yet do not sin; do not let the sun go down on your anger, and do not give the devil an opportunity." Allowing the "sun to go down on your wrath" means allowing bitterness and hatred to linger from day to day. As far as Paul is concerned, this gives the devil an opportunity. He loves bitterness because it is antithetical to God's grace. Yeshua taught us that if we have experienced forgiveness, we will also be ready to forgive others. When we refuse to forgive others, we are living as though we have not been forgiven ourselves, and our enemy likes that. Remember that in the Disciples' Prayer, Yeshua teaches us that God forgives our transgressions in the same manner that we forgive others. So exercising forgiveness is a very important thing!

As I have said, the antidote to bitterness and hatred is learning to forgive those who have hurt or offended us. Forgiving one another must be something that we are able and ready to do, meaning we must understand forgiveness and practice it regularly.

All of this pertains to relationships in general, and thus to marriage in particular. One might think that focusing on the act of forgiveness is to take a negative approach to marriage. Shouldn't we begin with the positive expectation that a husband and wife will treat each other with such love, that there will never be a need to forgive each other? Hardly! That would be like hoping the new car you buy really doesn't need oil because it is so well engineered. The reality of things is that we are all sinners saved by God's grace, and we all still wage war against the sinful nature. We are not perfect, and we are all growing and maturing in our faith—none of us have arrived yet! That also means that inevitably we will, at times, act selfishly, arrogantly, and without love. And that means we all will have opportunities to exercise forgiveness. This will be just as true in our marriages as it is in our work place, and our relationships with extended family members and friends.

A key biblical text dealing with forgiveness is Eph 4:31-32—

Greek	NASB
31 πᾶσα πικρία καὶ θυμὸς καὶ ὀργὴ καὶ κραυγὴ καὶ βλασφημία ἀρθήτω ἀφ᾽ ὑμῶν σὺν πάσῃ κακίᾳ. 32 γίνεσθε δὲ εἰς ἀλλήλους χρηστοί, εὔσπλαγχνοι, χαριζόμενοι ἑαυτοῖς, καθὼς καὶ ὁ θεὸς ἐν Χριστῷ ἐχαρίσατο ὑμῖν.	31 Let all bitterness and wrath and anger and clamor and slander be put away from you, along with all malice. 32 And be kind to one another, tender-hearted, forgiving each other, just as God in Messiah also has forgiven you.

As noted above, just prior to these verses, Paul has admonished us not to let the sun go down on our anger and thus to give opportunity to the devil. Here, he summarizes the bitter, unforgiving spirit with a list of terms (v. 31) and gives the command to be kind, and thus to forgive (v. 32). It can readily be seen that those things listed in v. 31 stand in opposition to kindness and the exercise of forgiveness. Thus, learning to forgive first involves recognizing and "putting away" those things that impede forgiveness. Let's look at each of the terms given in v. 31:

Bitterness   (πικρία, *pikria*) Involves the use of the tongue. This is insulting speech, belittling someone, making light of someone, either to his face or behind his back.

Wrath	(θυμὸς, *thumos*) An outburst of anger; quick flare-up; loss of temper; immediate retaliation
Anger	(ὀργὴ, *orge*) This is usually thought of as the "slow burn," the silent treatment. The word tends to convey a contemplative revenge.
Clamor	(κραυγὴ, *krauge*) Arguing, "a lot of noise," never letting the issue die; always bringing the matter up to the person's attention; needing to have the last word.
Slander	(βλασφημία, *blasphemia*) Literally, "blasphemy," degrading the character of someone; *lashon hara*
Malice	(κακία, *kakia*) Literally "bad things," and in this context, therefore, "bad feelings," "wrong motives." Every other kind of selfish or bad relational behavior.

The first important step in "putting away" these sinful behaviors is to recognize that they are, in fact, sin. We cannot excuse these things as just the function of our personalities or temperaments. While each of us will struggle with some of these more than others, we all must admit that they are contrary to what God wants of us, and we must therefore commit ourselves to put them away from our lives. These descriptions of sinful behavior simply cannot characterize us.

Then the Apostle gives us the positive exhortation to kindness and forgiveness in v. 32. And in so doing, he gives us the supreme example to follow, that is, the manner in which God forgave us in Messiah Yeshua. In fact, the language he uses is instructive: "...forgiving each other, *just as* (ὡς, *hos*) God in Messiah has forgiven you." Our forgiveness is to be patterned after God's forgiveness. The way He forgives is the way we are to forgive. It will be instructive, then, to study briefly the character and method of God's forgiveness in Yeshua.

1. God forgave us totally of His grace, not for self gain

God did not enrich Himself through forgiving us. On the contrary, forgiving us was very costly to Him. "For you know the grace of our Lord Yeshua Messiah, that though He was rich, yet for your sake He became poor, so that you through His poverty might become rich" (2Cor. 8:9). This is the very essence of love—a willingness to give without receiving. Selfish motives for extending forgiveness, or seeking it, betray a false forgiveness. Such feigned forgiveness is short-lived, and often breeds more strife.

2. God forgave us completely

    It is tempting to forgive in part and yet hold back a measure of the offense as a kind of advantage over the other person: "you still owe me because of what you did back then!" God doesn't remember our sins against us—He forgives them completely.
    Col. 2:13 When you were dead in your transgressions and the uncircumcision of your flesh, He made you alive together with Him, having forgiven us all our transgressions,
    Is. 55:7 Let the wicked forsake his way And the unrighteous man his thoughts; And let him return to the LORD, And He will have compassion on him, And to our God, For He will abundantly pardon.

3. God forgave us before we asked for forgiveness

    He forgave us when we did not deserve to be forgiven, even while we were still committing offenses against Him!
    Rom. 5:8 But God demonstrates His own love toward us, in that while we were yet sinners, Messiah died for us.

4. God forgave us on the basis of Messiah's death

    God did not forego His justice in order to forgive us. In other words, He didn't "sweep our sins under the carpet." Rather, He dealt with our sins by paying the penalty due to His justice. In this we learn that forgiveness is not antithetical to justice, but actually is the result of seeing justice served. Justice and forgiveness are two sides of the same coin.
    "For if while we were enemies we were reconciled to God through the death of His Son, much more, having been reconciled, we shall

be saved by His life" (Rom 5:10).

5. God's forgiveness is continual

> In 1John 1:9 we read: "If we confess our sins, He is faithful and righteous to forgive us our sins and to cleanse us from all unrighteousness." The Greek text gives us a little more insight into the Apostle's teaching. The opening verb, "confess," (ὁμολογῶμεν, *homologōmen*) is a present tense verb. We might translate it this way: "Whenever we confess our sins ...." That means that there is no limit to the number of times that we can come to God and ask for His forgiveness. And the verse goes on to say that whenever we confess our sins, God is faithful and righteous to forgives us. He is faithful, meaning He is always ready to forgive.
>
> Peter asked Yeshua a very interesting question about forgiveness in Matt 18:21–22: "Lord, how often shall my brother sin against me and I forgive him? Up to seven times?" Yeshua said to him, "I do not say to you, up to seven times, but up to seventy times seven." We should understand Yeshua's answer, not as a concrete arithmetic number, as though when we have forgiven 490 times, that's enough! No, seventy times seven was a way of saying "forgive as often as you are asked." This is exactly the way that God forgives us. Whenever we seek forgiveness, He is faithful *and* righteous to give us forgiveness.

So we may summarize God's way of forgiving us in Messiah as:
*   on the basis of His grace
*   completely
*   before we asked for forgiveness
*   in justice
*   continually

Now, since in Eph 4:32 Paul admonishes us to forgive in the same way that we are forgiven, we may take these characteristics of God's forgiveness as the model we are to follow.

Forgiving as a matter of grace

When someone sins against us, or offends us with unkind deeds, we must resist the tendency to offer forgiveness as a "down payment" for future actions. In other words, we should not forgive someone with the idea that when we do, that person is obligated toward us in ways that they otherwise would not be. Often, if such a motive is behind our "forgiveness," we hold out for a while, and really make the person squirm. We want them to know how much they have hurt us, and that when we finally do forgive them, they should understand that we're doing so as a big favor to them, and that we expect special favor on their part once we do give them our forgiveness. Or to put it another way, we should not use forgiveness as leverage to control the person we're forgiving. We don't forgive someone because they deserve to be forgiven. We forgive someone because we desire to obey God—because it is the right thing to do. God forgave us, not because we deserve to be forgiven, but because He is, by His very nature, a forgiving God.

There's another aspect to this: sometimes "forgiving" someone is to our advantage. We might feign forgiveness to someone who has something we want, or who has power to make things better for us. For instance, we may find it easier to let an offense go, when the one who has offended us holds a promotion in his power, or has something we want. But this is not true forgiveness—it's selfishness.

Yeshua teaches us that we are to forgive in the same way that we have been forgiven: "And forgive us our debts, as we also have forgiven our debtors" (Matt 6:12). In fact, it is when we have experienced the forgiveness of God that we are motivated to forgive others. Yeshua also teaches us this in His words about the woman who anointed His feet with perfume, and washed them with her tears. When the others were concerned about her actions, Yeshua responded: "For this reason I say to you, her sins, which are many, have been forgiven, for she loved much; but he who is forgiven little, loves little." A better translation would be: "...her sins, which are many, have been forgiven, *and the proof of this is* she loved much; but he who is forgiven little, loves little." In other words, when we come to appreciate the abundant, gracious forgiveness given to us by God in Messiah, we are compelled to forgive others in the same, gracious way.

Forgiving Completely

It is our natural tendency to withhold forgiveness as a way of controlling the situation, and especially as a way to protect ourselves. When someone hurts us by sinning against us, our natural response is to find a way not to be hurt by that person again, and often this is done by withholding full forgiveness. We can always tell when partial forgiveness exists, by the fact that we continue to bring up the offense. Complete forgiveness means that we no longer hold the offense as a weapon against the other person. We don't keep bringing up the past offense whenever we want to be in control. This does not mean that we forget the offense—that is often impossible. The Scriptures never command us to "forgive and forget," only to forgive. But when we do forgive someone, we discipline ourselves to put that offense away, and to reckon it as something that has been resolved. We resist the temptation of harboring an offense once it has been forgiven.

Once again, God's way of forgiveness is the model we are to follow. Consider Ps 103:12 – "As far as the east is from the west, so far has He removed our transgressions from us," and Col 2:13–14: "When you were dead in your transgressions and the uncircumcision of your flesh, He made you alive together with Him, having forgiven us all our transgressions, having canceled out the certificate of debt consisting of decrees against us, which was hostile to us; and He has taken it out of the way, having nailed it to the cross." God does not keep lists so that He can remind us of our sins. When He forgives us, He tears up the list and discards it. Paul describes love in this same way: 1Cor 13:5 "[Love] is not rude, it is not self-seeking, it is not easily angered, it keeps no record of wrongs" (NIV).

Forgiving before being asked to forgive

As we saw, God forgave us while we were still His enemy—before we ever asked His forgiveness. This becomes yet another aspect of how we are to forgive those who offend us.

It is natural to think that when someone offends us, it becomes our duty to "teach them a lesson" so they won't do it again. Logically, we think that if we extend forgiveness too quickly, the person will not take their sin against us seriously. Even more, we naturally think that withholding forgiveness will be a strong motivation for the person who has offended us to see the error of his or her ways. In this way, we make our forgiveness a reward for their repentance.

But this is just opposite of how things really work. We love God, not because we earned His forgiveness by our own sorrow over sin. We love God because we came to realize that He forgave us before we ever asked. In other words, we came to love Him because we understood that He had already loved us. Forgiving a person changes them—not withholding forgiveness. Withholding forgiveness only deepens the rift between the one offended and the offender, and opens the door for bitterness in the hearts of both.

This highlights an important fact about the nature of forgiveness itself: forgiveness is a change of attitude on the part of the one offended, not necessarily a restoration of relationship. Surely forgiveness smooths the way for a restored relationship, but it precedes restoration and is not dependent upon it. In other words, you can forgive someone whether or not your relationship to that person is ever fully restored. Forgiveness, then, is fundamentally a change of heart toward both the offense itself and the offender.

What is this change of attitude? First, we must confess the foundational truth that God is sovereign and in control of all things (Rom 8:28). We are not able to understand how the evil acts of people figure into the all-controlling sovereignty of God, but we know that somehow, in His infinite sovereignty, He is able to use even the sinful acts of men for His ultimate glory. This means that even when someone sins against us, we must trust that God can turn this for our good and His glory as we respond to the offense in righteous ways. So the first step in practicing forgiveness is to trust that God is in control, even in the situation that has caused us pain.

Secondly, we affirm the truth of God's word that He is the One who disciplines or punishes the sinner. Rom 12:19 "Do not take revenge, my friends, but leave room for God's wrath, for it is written: "It is mine to avenge; I will repay," says the Lord." Thus, when someone sins against me, it is not my place to see to it that he is punished or corrected. That is God's place. If I think that withholding forgiveness will punish the person by making them feel bad, I've usurped God's place as the avenger. So the second thing I must practice is giving the whole matter to God, and letting Him deal with it in His way and in His time. That means I give up any

notion I might have, that teaching the offender a lesson is my responsibility. My ability to change the person for the good will come by expressing
genuine forgiveness.

After affirming that God is the One who repays the sinner, Paul
goes on in Rom 12:20-21 to write: "On the contrary: 'If your enemy is
hungry, feed him; if he is thirsty, give him something to drink. In doing
this, you will heap burning coals on his head.' Do not be overcome by
evil, but overcome evil with good." The meaning of "heap burning coals
upon his head" (cf. Prov 25:22) is difficult to understand. Obviously, Paul
is not suggesting that the greatest revenge comes by being kind to those
who have sinned against us! If our motivation for kindness is revenge,
then the previous verse loses its entire force. Rather, the idea of "burning
coals" has the final judgement in view. In other words, if one is kind to
one's enemies, and this does not change them but they continue to act as
an enemy, then one's kindness will stand as yet another witness against
them in the final day. Ultimately, the point of Paul here is that revenge is
to be left in the hands of God, even if such revenge will not be meted out
until the judgment day.

Thirdly, forgiveness, as a change of attitude toward the offense
and the offender, allows one to view the whole situation from an entirely
different perspective. Once we have reckoned with the fact that God is in
control, even of this situation, and that He is the One Who is responsible
to correct and teach the offender, we are able to analyze the offense from
a different angle. More often than not, when a person sins against us, it
reveals a deeper need in their lives. For instance, a person often engages in
lashon hara because they feel inferior or marginalized. They think that by
bringing others down through gossip, they will elevate themselves. Once
we have given the situation to God, we are able to view the offense as an
indication of the offender's needs, and are therefore in a better position
genuinely to love that person by seeking to meet his or her needs. This
is especially true in the marriage relationship. Unkind words, disrespect,
anger, dishonesty—all of these are warning signs of much deeper needs.
Once we are able to change our attitude through applying forgiveness, we
can stop to ask the more important question: "what does this tell me about
the real needs of my spouse?" That is a love question! When we are able
to stop concerning ourselves with protecting ourselves, or getting revenge,
or teaching the offender a lesson, we are able to seek ways to help heal the
wounds that caused the offense in the first place.

Forgiving in the sphere of justice

We noted that God forgives us, not by sweeping our sins under the carpet, but by dealing with them in terms of satisfying His own, infinite justice. He did this by giving His Son, Yeshua, as payment for our sins. Thus, the forgiveness that He extends to us cost Him plenty!

We need to remember that forgiving someone does not mean pretending the offense didn't occur, or simply saying we won't talk about it any more—that is, leaving it unresolved and hoping that it will just go away. This is not forgiveness, and it will never solve the problem. Like a sliver that is left under the skin, an unresolved offense will just continue to fester. Yeshua teaches us that when offenses occur, we are to be active in resolving the conflict: Matt. 5:23–24, "Therefore, if you are offering your gift at the altar and there remember that your brother has something against you, leave your gift there in front of the altar. First go and be reconciled to your brother; then come and offer your gift." Here, "be reconciled" does not mean "have your relationship restored." It means that you do all in your power to right the wrong, whether or not the person you have sinned against acknowledges it. At the minimum, this means you ask for his or her forgiveness. It means that you engage in restoration of whatever material things may have been the cause of the offense. From the side of the one offended, it means that you willingly forgive, and that you accomplish what needs to be done in order to rectify the wrong.

So forgiveness is not devoid of justice: it depends upon it. Only when wrongs have been righted, can there be any hope of restoring the relationship. But it is important to realize that when you have done all you can do (asked forgiveness, restored whatever you are able), you have fulfilled your obligation. If the person refuses to say he or she forgives you, that is their problem, not yours. You may return to the "altar" and "offer your gift."

There is one other aspect of this characteristic of forgiveness, as it pertains to extending forgiveness to a fellow believer. We should remember that God has already forgiven the person of his or her sin through the sacrifice of Yeshua. He has declared that person righteous. If God has forgiven all of our sins in Yeshua, who are we to withhold forgiveness? Are we more righteous than God Himself?! So a further motivation in forgiving someone who has sinned against us, is to remember that God has already forgiven him or her. Moreover, since the death of Yeshua is the final and ultimate basis for forgiveness of sins, we may forgive those who sin against us on the same grounds. If Yeshua died to pay the penalty of the very sin enacted against us by someone, then what right do we have to hold the offense as though it still needs to be paid?

Forgiving Continually

One of the hardest things to do is to continue to forgive someone when they repeatedly sin against us. We begin to think that in forgiving the person, we are simply enabling them to continue in their sin. We're "letting them off the hook," when we should be holding their feet to the fire by telling them "this is the last time I'm forgiving you for this. If it happens again, forget it!" But, as I've noted above, it is not our place to bring justice upon the head of the one who has sinned against us. That is God's responsibility. Moreover, withholding forgiveness does not change the person who has sinned against us, it only hardens them. But most importantly, withholding forgiveness opens the way in our own hearts for bitterness.

Once again, however, I want to make it clear that forgiveness does not dismiss justice. Let me relate a story to try to illustrate this. A family I know went through a terrible tragedy. A prowler broke into the home of their daughter, and in the course of the theft, was startled by the daughter walking into the room, and subsequently shot and killed her. The sorrow, anger, and dismay that the whole family felt was understandable. A great injustice had been committed, and there was no way to rectify the wrong that had been done. The parents asked me, in the course of time, how they could deal with the bitterness and hatred they felt for the criminal. They admitted that, while they were dealing with the sorrow of the loss of their daughter, the bitterness against her assailant was eating them up inside. As difficult as it was, I began to tell them about their need to forgive him. At first, that sounded strange to me as well. How could anyone forgive such a person who had brought so great a sorrow upon this family? But then I explained that forgiving him meant putting him into the hands of God, and letting God deal with how justice would be served. In time, they understood this and were able to let go of the bitterness by exercising forgiveness. But then the trial took place, and they asked me how they should feel toward the criminal they had forgiven. Should they pray that he might be given a light sentence, or that he might even be acquitted of the crime? Here I reminded them that God, Who is fully merciful while at the same time just, had already decreed that a murderer deserved the death penalty. *Their willingness to forgive the criminal did not negate that he should pay for his crime in accordance with God's justice.* In the midst of having forgiven him, meaning they had removed themselves from the need to take revenge, they could still trust that God would administer justice in accordance with His own righteousness.

How does this principle apply in our everyday lives and relationships? It means that while we commit ourselves to an unending practice of forgiveness, we do not negate the need to see justice is met. A wife whose husband is unfaithful, should commit herself to forgive him. But even after engaging in genuine forgiveness, she still has the right, in accordance with God's justice, to seek a divorce from him. The two things are not mutually exclusive. This highlights the fact that forgiveness and restoration of a broken relationship are not necessarily the same. Forgiveness may lead to restoration, and that, of course, is the best outcome. But forgiveness is fundamentally a change of heart in the one who has been offended. Restoration is the willingness and the ability to rebuild what has been broken through sin, and this involves both parties.

Roadblocks to Forgiveness, or Attitudes of an Unforgiving Heart

Let's face it: forgiving someone who has hurt us is one of the hardest things we do. That is because forgiveness is contrary to our sinful nature. If we allow our sinful nature to lead the way, we will always find very good reasons why we should withhold forgiveness. Moreover, the enemy of our souls hates forgiveness. Since our battle is not against people, but against the evil powers (Eph 6:12), when we commit ourselves to obey God, we are engaged in a spiritual battle as well. This is all the more true in the area of forgiveness. The enemy knows that his primary foothold in the lives of people is bitterness, and he also knows that exercising the spiritual duty of forgiveness dispels bitterness. So given the opportunity, he will set all manner of roadblocks in the path of anyone who is committed to extending forgiveness.

1. "I'm trying to forgive, but I just can't forget what he/she has done to me!"

As I noted above, there is no Scriptural requirement to forget in order to forgive. One does not forget what has taken place; one changes their attitude toward the one who has caused the offense.

Yeshua teaches this when He gave the parable to His disciples, following Peter's question about how often we should forgive someone who has sinned against us (Matt 18:23ff). In this parable, a king is settling accounts with his servants. He brings before him one man who owed ten thousand talents and demands that he pay his debt. Unable to come up with that amount of money, the master demands that he, his wife, and children be sold into slavery to pay the debt. With nothing left to do but beg for the master's mercies, the servant falls to his knees and pleads his cause. The story goes to tell that the master felt pity upon the man, and *forgave* his debt and let him go free. Now free from his burden, the servant went out and found someone who owed him money, and demanded payment. When the man could not repay the debt, the servant demanded that he be thrown in prison. This turn of events was reported back to the king, who immediately summoned the unworthy servant, reprimanded him, and reinstated his debt. He sent the unworthy servant to prison until such time as the debt was fully paid.

Here, in the parable, we see that the king forgave the debt initially, but he did not forget it! When the servant acted unworthily, the debt was easily reinstated.

The same is true of the New Covenant text in Jer 31:31-34. Here, God says regarding the sins of Israel, "For I will forgive their wickedness and will remember their sins no more." But in this context, the word "remember" is used in a covenant sense, meaning "I will forgive their sins and no longer credit them to their account." Obviously, the all-knowing God cannot "forget" anything! The point of forgiveness, from a divine perspective, is that the sins are no longer credited or charged to the account of the sinner.

So remembering the offense should not be a roadblock to forgiving it. Rather, forgiveness exists in the willingness to consider the debt (offense) paid in full. It is a change of attitude toward the offense and the offender.

2. "He needs to learn a lesson! He hurt me, and I'm not about to forgive him until he understands how much pain he caused."

Revenge is probably at the heart of an unforgiving attitude. But as we have seen, revenge belongs to God, not to us. When our hearts lean toward harboring unforgiveness because we want to "even the scales" with the one who has hurt us, we must remember that in doing so, we are usurping God's rightful place as the Judge of all the earth.

Furthermore, revenge is a single way of describing those things listed in Eph 4:31, the very things that we are commanded to "put away" in order to exercise forgiveness. Revenge is the opposite of love, and Paul teaches us that "love does not take revenge" (1Cor 13:5). In the end, revenge is selfishness. We may try to convince ourselves that revenge is the enactment of justice, but if we attempt to bring about justice in unjust ways, we actually have thwarted justice.

We also should reckon with the fact that if revenge was the way to deal with sin, we all would fall before the wrath of God. Instead, God, in His mercy, extended forgiveness to us in spite of the fact that we had sinned against Him. If our hearts are attracted to revenge when someone sins against us, it is time to rehearse once again how God forgave us, and to revel in the glory of His love. When we have experienced His forgiveness and love afresh, we will be far more able to extend forgiveness and love to the one who has sinned against us.

Likewise, we should remember that when we take revenge as our duty, we have taken to ourselves what rightfully belongs to God. This is a very dangerous step, because thinking we can act in God's place is the very substance of Satan's rebellion from the beginning. He wanted to be "like God." A heart set on revenge is a heart governed by bitterness, and bitterness gives way to the devil. Whenever we begin to plan revenge, we should be awakened to the fact that we are giving into the very ways of the enemy.

3. "As soon as he asks for forgiveness, I'll give it to him, and not a second before!"

This roadblock to forgiveness is founded upon the common misunderstanding of what forgiveness is in the first place. Forgiveness is not something that is earned by one's seeking it, or warranted by one's repentance. What if the person who sinned against you never asks for your forgiveness? Does that mean you harbor ill feelings against him or her for the rest of your life? What good would that do either for yourself or for the one who has sinned against you? It only leaves you harboring an offense, and vulnerable to bitterness.

Here is where Paul's admonition to forgive "just as God forgave" us in Yeshua is insightful. Just as God forgave us before we ever sought forgiveness, so we are able to forgive those who sin against us before they ever approach us for forgiveness. Remember, forgiveness means 1) believing that God is in control of every situation, meaning that He has the ability to take your current situation and turn it to His glory and your good, 2) confessing that God is the One Who is in charge of the person who has sinned against you, and He is the One who will administer discipline or punishment, and teach that person what he or she needs to learn, and 3) the offense against you can be used to understand the deeper issues and problems of the offender, giving you the ability to love them in genuine ways.

These steps to forgiveness, which are really nothing more than agreeing with God and acting upon what He has said, can be done well before the offender ever seeks your forgiveness. In fact, they should be! The sooner we can move toward forgiveness, the better. Don't leave any time for bitterness to grow and take root. When someone sins against you, begin the process of forgiveness. Then if and when that person comes to seek your forgiveness, you will be fully able to offer it without reservations.

4. "He's not sincere when he asks me to forgive him! The reason I know, is that he's done this before, and I think he'll probably do it again. He's just taking advantage of my kindness!"

As we have seen, Yeshua teaches us that we are to keep on forgiving, regardless of how many times someone sins against us. So the choice is not whether I should forgive or not, but whether I will obey or not. The idea that if I withhold forgiveness from someone who continues to sin against me, this will rectify the situation, is wrong headed. Withholding forgiveness is itself a sin, and one cannot overcome sin with sin.

Once again, however, this roadblock stems from a misunderstanding of what forgiveness is in the first place. Forgiveness is the change of attitude on the part of the one who has been offended. It's primary effect is not on the one who has caused the offense, but upon the heart of the one offended. Forgiving frees the heart to "love your enemies, do good to those who hate you, bless those who curse you, pray for those who mistreat you" (Lk 6:27). In other words, forgiveness frees a person to follow in the footsteps of Yeshua.

What to expect if you commit yourself to exercising forgiveness

I wish it were possible to promise that when we commit ourselves to forgiving those who hurt us, we will always experience happiness and success without trials! But we all know that is not the case in this fallen world. If we do follow in the footsteps of Yeshua, and love those who hurt us as He commanded, we can expect that there will be some measure of suffering. Forgiveness is an act of love, and love means giving oneself away. That, too, is contrary to our sin nature, and that means we will have to die to self in order to forgive.

But what can we expect as the outcome of exercising forgiveness toward those who offend us? First, people may consider us weak, and think they can take advantage of us all the more. We may be diminished in the eyes of some, because we are not willing to slander the one who has sinned against us, because we have already forgiven that person. But our strength is in the Lord. We leave the outcome of obeying Him in His hands. Secondly, we may be slandered. People who are bent to revenge and bitterness will consider our willingness to forgive as a character flaw—an inability to "stand up for our rights." This may particularly be the case in the workplace, where slander and revenge is the common stock and trade. Thirdly, and most importantly, we should expect success in our own lives, because God promises to bless those who obey Him. And forgiveness is first and foremost a matter of obedience to our Master. A forgiving heart is one that is at rest with the Lord and with itself. Self-contentment is a rare treasure, and one that should be highly prized. Being able to go to sleep at night, knowing that no bitterness or revenge is harbored in one's heart, is a great delight. Moreover, obeying God by forgiving those who sin against us keeps our hearts pure before the Almighty. Withholding forgiveness means harboring sin in our hearts. The bitterness that an unforgiving heart nurtures is a cancer that will eventually affect one's entire outlook and perspective on life. Practicing forgiveness therefore frees the heart to fervent worship, a joyful spirit, and the ability to enjoy all of the good things God has given us. Finally, a person who knows how to forgive is a vessel fit for the Master's use. He is not self-consumed with the way others have hurt him, because he has placed these situations into the Almighty's hands, and is content to leave them there. He is not constantly burdened with the offenses of others, and is therefore able to bear the burdens of others, and in so doing, to fulfill the Torah of Messiah (Gal 6:2).

Let's Talk About It

1. Why is it important to let go of bitterness? What happens if one allows bitterness to remain in one's heart or mind?

2. What are some of the steps you should take to start to forgive someone who has hurt you?

3. What do we do when we know we should forgive someone, but they haven't asked for forgiveness?

4. Can we forgive someone that is no longer in our lives? If so, how does this work?

5. Explain how forgiving someone who has hurt you does not necessarily mean that the relationship is restored. Or the question could be asked this way: How is it possible to forgive someone for the wrong they have done against you and still not have the relationship restored?

6. Should we forgive someone if we're pretty sure they'll do the same thing again?

Chapter 10
Husband & Wife: Intimate Friends

In Chapter Five, we looked at some basic characteristics of a Godly husband under the headings of faithfulness, caring, leading, and communicating. In the next chapter, we noted some of the characteristics of a Godly wife, emphasizing spiritual strength, beauty, respect, and the model of the *Eshet Chail* of Proverbs 31. In this chapter, we want to look at some important practical aspects of the marriage relationship—the kinds of things that build friendship and intimacy.

Obviously, there are many different levels of friendship. The word "friend" in our modern world carries a wide range of meanings. In the most general sense, a friend may simply be someone who is not an enemy. Or, a friend may be someone we see occasionally. Usually, however, we describe a person as our friend as someone with whom we have a close relationship built upon common interests and a mutual sharing of things we consider most important. Friendship is based upon a mutual commitment to that friendship, built upon a growing trust of each other. Our closest friends are those with whom we have made the deepest commitments, and with whom we have found unbroken trust. When either commitment or trust are diminished, so is our friendship.

This means, of course, that marriage ought to foster the deepest of all friendships. But commitment and trust are not guaranteed by-products of a marriage contract—they must be nurtured and strengthened. When either a husband or a wife acts in such a way so as to diminish trust, or in such a way as to appear less than committed to the marriage, fractures occur. And if these are not quickly and effectively repaired, bigger troubles are in store. As we noted in the previous chapter, learning to practice the spiritual *mitzvah* of forgiveness is the first step in the repairing process.

God intends that a husband and wife be close companions. Indeed, He ordained that they should be the closest of friends. The ability of a man and his wife to become one forms an exclusive companionship—a friendship that exists on all levels: spiritual, emotional, and physical. In fact, the physical oneness within marriage is designed to be an expression of the spiritual and emotional companionship that already exists. But it is more than merely an expression of an already existing companionship. The physical relationship of oneness enhances and strengthens the spiritual and emotional relationship of mutual commitment.

God created us as sexual beings. He created us with a desire for each other as male and female. And He did so for very good reasons. This means that sexual desires are not evil—they are God-given. They only become evil when they are used in a way that God never intended. We all know that it is always the plan of the enemy to turn what God created as beautiful into something ugly.

Some have taught that the primary reason God put sexual desires within us was to insure the procreation of children. Frankly, I find that hard to believe. If God had wanted simply to ensure that couples would have children, He could have done it in a million other ways. Procreation could have been accomplished entirely devoid of emotion or feeling. But had that been the case, a very important aspect of the whole process would have been missing. This is the aspect of joy that was to accompany the ability to procreate.

God made the sexual act one of pleasure, and He did so for a number of reasons. Primary was the fact that in the physical union between a husband and wife, His own desire and joy for His bride was to be expressed. In like manner, the sense of being entirely encompassed by a gentle, caressing husband portrays the joy we have as we experience the faithful, sustaining hand of our Master. In the ultimate sense, the sexual relationship in marriage was given to reveal the mutual love and companionship that exists between Yeshua and His bride, and as such, it takes on even greater sanctity.

Yet another reason exists for why God created the physical relationship within marriage to be one of mutual joy and satisfaction. Since children are often the result of the sexual relationship, they are to be seen as yet another aspect of the joy that the physical relationship brings. Children are a blessing from God! And even though they require a great deal of sacrifice on the part of parents, they teach us much about what actually constitutes joy in this life.

It is right, then, that a husband and wife are drawn to each other physically. Moreover, the physical relationship within marriage entails far more than the sexual act itself. An affectionate glance, holding hands, walking arm-in-arm, hugging, kissing—these and more are all physical signs of affection that naturally occur within a healthy marriage relationship.

So if sexual relations within marriage are both ordained by God, and the desire for such a physical relationship is created within us, why do so many married couples have difficulty in this area? Some statistics indicate that sexual dissatisfaction between husbands and wives ranks second only to financial difficulties as the driving cause of divorce. There are several reasons for this. First, many married couples have never considered the sexual relationship within marriage from God's perspective. They have viewed sex as a personal right, and a means to self-satisfaction. In short, their view of the sexual relationship is selfish. For them, fulfilling their own needs is the goal of the sexual relationship. The problem with this is not only that such a view wrests the sexual relationship from its divinely intended purpose, but that selfishness is never satisfied. Selfishness is a cancer that grows with every feeding. So when marriage partners view their physical relationship as a means to satisfying their own desires, they will inevitably be disappointed. Rather, each partner must develop the perspective that their goal in the physical relationship must be to please and fulfill the other. At first, such a suggestion might seem to mitigate against the idea of pleasure itself. Isn't pleasure, by its very nature, self-fulfilling? Yet God's ways are not our ways. What we discover is that when we put the other person's needs ahead of our own, we end up deriving pleasure we never would have suspected. This is a wide-ranging principle, but it is also applicable in the physical relationship of marriage. When a husband learns to find genuine joy in fulfilling the sexual needs of his wife, he will at the same time discover abundant joy himself. Likewise, in such a scenario, a wife who desires to please her caring husband, will find a deep and fulfilling satisfaction in the physical relationship. This is not the way of the world, but it is God's way.

Principles from the Song of Songs

Contained in the canon of our Scriptures is *Shir HaShirim*, or Song of Songs. Throughout the centuries, many different interpretations of this love poem have been offered. The majority of Christian commentators, particularly those in past centuries, have interpreted the poem allegorically, as describing the love of Messiah for His bride. In this interpretation, they borrowed a similar allegorical interpretation of the Sages who often interpreted the book as a metaphor of God's love for Israel, His bride. Yet it seems clear that the book is a love poem, and describes, in very cryptic and poetic terms, the relationship of a husband and his wife. The fact that it was retained within the canon, proving its self-authenticating worth, shows, in my opinion, the sacred nature and value of the physical relationship within marriage. This is not to deny the many exegetical difficulties that the book presents. It is only to say that in the broadest of strokes, Song of Songs remains as the inspired revelation of God's heart toward the intimacy of marriage.

Principle 1: *The sexual act within marriage is not an end in itself. The morning after is just as important, and maybe more important.*

I derive this principle from the overall structure of the Song. The book as a whole is constructed in chiastic arrangement, meaning that the beginning of chapter 1 mirrors the ending of chapter 8, and so on, until one comes to the middle of the book, which is 5:1, "I have come into my garden, my sister, my bride," a phrase that poetically describes the sexual act. If we were to give a broad outline of the book, it might look like this:
I. Introduction and Courtship (1:1–3:5)
II. Wedding and Consummation (3:6–5:1)
III. Maturity of Marriage and Conclusion (5:2–8:14)

Thus, the structure of the book itself reminds us of this very important principle: the physical relationship in marriage is not the goal of marriage. Nor should it be the reason for marriage. It is one means by which a growing, maturing love develops within the marriage. Thus, if the physical relationship in marriage becomes the primary focus, it has lost its proper place and function.

Principle 2: *The physical relationship in marriage requires preparation.*

The opening description of the bride tells us about her physical appearance:

1:6 "Do not stare at me because I am swarthy, For the sun has burned me. My mother's sons were angry with me; They made me caretaker of the vineyards, But I have not taken care of my own vineyard.

She describes herself as plain and rough from work in the fields. She has neglected her own grooming as she groomed the vineyards. Yet in the following context she seeks to perfume herself, and to make herself beautiful for her lover. She is not content to remain in her "work clothes," for she desires to attract the eyes of her beloved. The same is true of the groom (3:6ff). He is "perfumed with myrrh and frankincense" when he arrives. He comes with the strength of manliness, yet prepared and groomed for his bride.

In the poetry of the Song, we see how right it is for a husband and wife to prepare themselves for each other. During courtship days, a young man and women take extra time and care to present themselves as attractive to each other. Unfortunately, this is often forgotten after the passing of years in marriage. But it should not be. God intended that a man should be attracted to the beauty of his wife, and that he should prepare himself to be fitting for her beauty.

Dr. Laura, speaking to wives, puts it this way:

> What attracts men to women is their femininity, and femininity isn't only about appearance, it's also about behaviors. Looking womanly and behaving sweetly and flirtatiously are gifts wives give to their husbands. This gift communicates that the husband is seen as a man, not just a fix-it guy, the bread-winner, or the sperm donor. And if it's romancing a wife is hungering for, presenting oneself as an appealing "woman" will get more romancing than presenting oneself as only a child-care worker, or house cleaner, or the other wage earner. (*The Proper Care and Feeding of Husbands*, p. 121).

Men, we also need to take a cue from Solomon's love poem. Granted, he was the King, and spared no expense for his lavish wardrobe and furnishings. But there's no reason why we can't present ourselves as kings in our own homes. When we neglect common grooming, constantly show up in tattered work clothes, and treat common manners as something that no longer matter—we're not presenting ourselves as worthy men. When a man takes his wife out for dinner, and crawls into bed with her afterwards, she ought to see in him the same kind of man who took every measure to be attractive to her when they were courting.

In reality, husbands and wives who stop trying to be attractive to each other are subtly sending the message that they take each other for granted. No one wants to be taken for granted, and in fact, friends don't take each other for granted. Husbands and wives who want to honor God in their physical relationship and through it, to grow deeper in their companionship, will do well to remain attractive to each other.

Principle 3: *Romance is an essential part of the physical relationship*

Throughout the Song, we read the words of the bride and groom describing each other. They speak of each other's beautiful or handsome features, of the excitement of being together, and their longing for each other when apart. Primarily in the Song, these words are directed to each other, not to others (though they speak highly about each other to their friends as well). In other words, they talk to each other in romantic ways, and they do things for each other that have romantic overtones.

Let's face it, though. Men and women define romance differently. When a man wants to romance his wife, he thinks of saying sweet words, buying her flowers or perfume, taking her out to dinner, or getting some other gift that would please her. But when a man dreams about his wife being romantic, he's not thinking she might buy him a new DeWalt power pack or a scope for his favorite hunting rifle. A man thinks more of how his wife presents herself to him as a woman, expressing her desire for him as a competent man.

Likewise, just getting gifts for your wife isn't necessarily romantic. Along with the gift, or the night out, she desires to be treated as a woman and cared for like a princess. She needs to know that as far as you are concerned, she is "altogether beautiful" (Song 4:7), and that you are fully satisfied with her as your closest companion and lover.

This means that romance within a marriage is expressed in many small yet significant gestures, words, and actions, not just an occasional night out on the town. In many ways, the joy of the physical relationship should be the crowning jewel in an ongoing romance of daily life together.

Principle 4: *Your spouse's needs should take a priority over your own.*

In one section of the Song (5:2–6), a sexual scene is described in poetic, veiled terms. The groom had come to his bride, but she was not ready for him. She awoke only after he had knocked, but when she opened the door, he had already left. Throughout the poem (e.g., 8:4), he gives instructions not to awaken his beloved until she is ready.

This is all poetic imagery to teach a very important lesson: the physical relationship must take into account the readiness of both partners. Entering into love making as though it is a duty rather than a pleasure diminishes its pleasure and value. This is where understanding and genuine love must prove itself, because being open with each other about fears, desires (or lack thereof), apprehensions, or even unexplained feelings, is very difficult. In the Song, the groom does not begrudge the fact that his bride is not ready for his advances. He leaves and gives her time and space to become ready. In portraying this scenario, the Song highlights a reality: a man's sexual drive is usually stronger than a woman's, meaning that usually a husband will desire sexual relations more often than his wife does. But the Song also gives a pattern for what a man should do when his wife is not ready. He should give her time and space, and affirm that he does not begrudge her needs, but rather has her needs as the most important priority in his heart.

Wives, on the other hand, should recognize that their husbands will have stronger desires sexually, and they ought to seek to fulfill their husband's needs as they are able.

> In order for a wife to do that, she's got to tune out of herself and tune in to him. For many wives it means tossing out their bags of petty, bitter feelings, resentments, disappointments, and overreactions to basic annoyances. While that is often a daunting task, the rewards are worth it in the long run. (*The Proper Care and Feeding of Husbands*, p. 123)

Many factors can disrupt the physical relationship between a husband and a wife. Medical issues are often at the root of sexual dysfunction. A willingness to admit that there is a problem is the first step to searching out possible medical solutions. Some people may have long term issues that stem from childhood. Woman who have been abused or raped as young girls will bear emotional scars that are very difficult to overcome.[1] These kinds of tragic events will have a tremendous impact on their ability to accept and enjoy the physical aspects of love in a marriage. Yet, given time and understanding, and a willingness to work through the issues, they can overcome the abuse of their past, and experience true freedom in their marriage relationship. Key to such success will be the patience and care shown by a loving and understanding husband. But this will require that a husband put the needs of his wife ahead of his own

---

1. A book that may be very helpful for those who have been abused as children is: *The Wounded Heart: Hope for Adult Victims of Childhood Sexual Abuse* by Dan B. Allender

needs, regardless of how legitimate his own needs may be.

These are just four principles derived from the Song—there are many more! We would do well, as husbands and wives, to often rehearse the love poetry of the Song, and allow it to teach us more and more of God's heart regarding the physical relationship He has ordained for marriage.

1Corinthians 7:1–5

In the opening verses of 1Cor 7, Paul gives some straightforward admonitions regarding the physical relationship in marriage.

> 1 Now concerning the things about which you wrote, it is good for a man not to touch a woman. 2 But because of immoralities, each man is to have his own wife, and each woman is to have her own husband. 3 The husband must fulfill his duty to his wife, and likewise also the wife to her husband. 4 The wife does not have authority over her own body, but the husband does; and likewise also the husband does not have authority over his own body, but the wife does. 5 Stop depriving one another, except by agreement for a time, so that you may devote yourselves to prayer, and come together again so that Satan will not tempt you because of your lack of self-control.

First, Paul teaches that at least one aspect of the physical relationship within marriage is that it is a means of sanctification—it aids both the husband and the wife in the area of sexual purity. This is because as a husband and wife are fulfilled with each other, they will be less tempted to look elsewhere for fulfillment. Thus, the physical relationship of husband and wife is considered by the Apostle as a "duty." By this we should not understand some perfunctory performance apart from a proper desire. Like any of the *mitzvot,* we should consider the sexual relationship within marriage as a happy fulfillment of God's will, and expect His blessing and favor as a result of our obedience. In like manner, we should recognize that withholding ourselves from our spouse not only is contrary to God's will, but it may be spiritually detrimental as well.

Secondly, in making this admonition, Paul clearly forbids that husbands or wives should use the physical relationship within their marriage as a way to control each other. A wife who gets her way by promising physical love is abusing a most precious and sacred *mitzvah.* Likewise, a husband is not free to demand that his wife engage in physical relations whenever he desires. *Each of them is the authority over the other.* The only way this can work is if each of them willingly submits to the other. All too often, men have taken this passage to mean that they can demand physical relations with their wife. But those who do so fail to recognize that the Apostle gives her equal authority in the situation. Paul's solution to what might seem an impasse is simple: "Stop depriving each other." This means that the physical relationship within marriage must be an extension of the willingness of both to meet the needs of the other. Where there is a genuine willingness to meet each others needs, the wife will not be forced against her will, and the husband will be fulfilled with his wife.

Thirdly, this passage indicates that abstaining from sexual relations within the marriage may be done by mutual consent of the husband and wife, but that such a scenario should only be for a short time, and then only for the purpose of devoting oneself to prayer. If we understand this against the context of 1st Century Israel, when the Temple still stood, it may have been that Paul recognized the need to remain ritually or ceremonially clean during certain days of the *mo'edim*, when regular attendance at the Temple (prayers) would take precedence over physical relations, which would have rendered the couple ceremonially unclean until evening. By extension of this principle, it may be appropriate to cease sexual relations within a marriage for a short period of time in order to give oneself to a particularly important religious duty, but as noted, this should be only for a "time," with the full intension of coming back together in the normal physical relations of marriage.

Finally, this passage highlights another important reality. Husbands and wives should expect to find their fulfillment in each other. A man who succumbs to pornography, for instance, is seeking some measure of sexual fulfillment outside of his marriage. In doing so, he is taking a first step toward adultery, fulfilling the lusts of his flesh rather than seeking to fulfill his wife, by which he would find fulfillment himself. Likewise, a woman who flirts with other men is seeking some measure of fulfillment outside of her marriage. What may seem to her as a kind of innocent fun, is in reality playing with fire. A wife should save all of her flirtation for her husband—it rightfully belongs to him.

Summary

The physical relationship in marriage is a God-given gift of joy and pleasure. It is a revelation of God's own passion toward His bride, and of the manner in which His people are satisfied with Him. In the same way that a husband is honored when his wife is satisfied in him, so God is most honored when we are most satisfied in Him.

The physical relationship in marriage is, however, not an end in itself. It is a means to the greater goal of friendship or companionship. Thus, a husband and wife must consider the needs of each other as more important than their own needs. The physical relationship is one of mutual care and concern for each other, and a means of expressing the deepest commitment and trust in each other.

From the Song of Songs, we derived four principles:

1. *The sexual act within marriage is not an end in itself. The morning after is just as important, and maybe more important.*
Sexual relations within marriage should never become the primary focus. The physical relationship is a deep, intimate expression of the love and care a husband and wife have for each other.

2. *The physical relationship in marriage requires preparation.*
Husbands and wives should strive to be attractive to each other, which further enhances their physical relationships

3. *Romance is an essential part of the physical relationship.*
The physical relationship is the crowning jewel in an ongoing romance of daily life together.

4. *Your spouse's needs should take a priority over your own.*
The goal in the physical relationship of marriage should be to satisfy and fulfill the needs of your spouse. This means that his or her needs are more important than your own desires.

The principles are further substantiated by Paul in 1Cor 7:1–5, in which he teaches that the physical relationship in marriage is a sacred duty (*mitzvah*) by which both the husband and wife are sanctified unto God.

Let's Talk About It

1. If the physical relationship in marriage is ordained by God and therefore of high importance, why is it often difficult for parents to discuss these matters with their children? How can these difficulties be overcome?

2. Share some of the methods you have used to help teach your children a biblical view of sexuality. How old were your children when you began to teaching them about these important things? What materials did you find helpful?

3. Would you consider your spouse to be your closest friend? What kinds of things can you do to build and strengthen your friendship?

4. Why is it important to keep myself physically attractive to my spouse? After all, we're already married!

5. Throughout the Song of Songs, romance is seen as an essential part of the physical relationship. Consider how to build more romance into your marriage.

www.ingramcontent.com/pod-product-compliance
Lightning Source LLC
Chambersburg PA
CBHW060229030426
42335CB00014B/1382